The Greatest of These

is

Love

The Greatest of These is *Love*

GLENDA HAINES

TATE PUBLISHING
AND ENTERPRISES, LLC

Published by Tate Publishing & Enterprises, LLC
127 E. Trade Center Terrace | Mustang, Oklahoma 73064 USA
1.888.361.9473 | www.tatepublishing.com

Tate Publishing is committed to excellence in the publishing industry. The company reflects the philosophy established by the founders, based on Psalm 68:11,
"The Lord gave the word and great was the company of those who published it."

Book design copyright © 2012 by Tate Publishing, LLC. All rights reserved.
Cover design by Jan Sunday Quilaquil
Interior design by Caypeeline Casas

Published in the United States of America

ISBN: 978-1-62147-453-1
1. Religion / Christian Life / Devotional
2. Religion / Christian Life / Spiritual Growth
12.10.10

DEDICATION

This book is dedicated to the congregation of my home church in Lakewood, Colorado, in appreciation for their prayers and support of this writing.

TABLE OF CONTENTS

Introduction 9
The Father's Love Revealed in Creation.............. 15
Perfect Love in Balance 35
The Father's Love in the Old Testament............. 48
Jesus: Our Example of Love................... 69
What Is Love? 93
The Holy Spirit: God's Love in Us.................... 112
Suffering 133
Love Versus Fear 146
Love Versus the Flesh 170
Love Versus Unforgiveness 197
Love Versus Demonic Activity.............. 215
The Love of the Father........................ 233

INTRODUCTION

*W*hat is the Father's love? How can we begin to comprehend the perfect and complete love that God has for His children? How deep and real is that love for you as an individual? In this writing, we will explore these questions and more.

Our journey will begin with discovering the Father's love in creation. We are now all born into an imperfect world, but it was not that way in the beginning. God created a perfect world without flaws. Sin, abuse, hate, rejection, and crime did not exist. There was only love, beauty, and perfection. Everything was pure in every sense and form.

God's original plan and intent for man begins to unfold as we see the creation process. The drama of life continues as we see the creation of man who was made in the image of God. The heavenly Father then gives His greatest creation (man) dominion over the earth, which He had created in complete perfection.

What went wrong? The heavenly Father desired to have a family who would, of their own free will, love and serve Him. He did not want to withhold any good thing from them but wanted mankind to share in His kingdom. However, true love cannot be commanded but is a choice that is made by one's own free will. This brings us to the Garden of Eden and the tree of the knowledge of good and evil.

Adam and Eve were to be the caretakers of the Garden of Eden. They could enjoy everything in the garden and eat of every tree but of the tree of the knowledge of good and evil. Adam and Eve, who represented the future of mankind, would be able to make a choice to love and serve God or disobey God and choose their own path. They chose to disobey God and we are, to this day, still living in the wake and consequences of their decision.

God does not give up on His creation. True love never fails, and the love of the Father did not fail mankind even when mankind failed God.

God continued in hope and love to help mankind recover from their sin in the Garden of Eden while still giving mankind a way to make the right choices that would bring them back to Himself. In order to understand this kind of love, we must explore God's two distinct natures that has been revealed to us.

God's love is in perfect balance, and He wants to reveal His nature to us so we can better understand and serve Him. His ways are higher than our ways and, too often, we want to bring Him down to our level of thinking. Instead, God wants to bring us up to *His* level of thinking. The heavenly Father looks at us through the eyes of eternity. Our lives consist of more than just the vapor of life that we live here on earth. God has given us choices to make, and we are responsible for those choices. A loving father will and can discipline his children to keep them on the right path and out of trouble. This can be painful in the short term but an act of love for the long term. Have you ever been taken to the spiritual woodshed? This is the kind of love that will last forever, and this is who God is.

For some, the Old Testament in the Bible reflects an angry God. It seems as if God is mad all the time. However, that is not true. We will examine the love of God that is demonstrated in His dealings with the children of Israel, as well as the story of Balaam and Balack. God goes to great length to protect His people as well as protect the bloodline that will bring forth the Messiah. Also, we will discuss Hosea and his relationship with a harlot named Gomer. Their marriage was a type and shadow of the relationship between Israel and God. Israel was like a wandering, unfaithful harlot, and God was the loving, faithful husband who pursued His unfaithful wife.

The sacrifice of Jesus on the cross is the greatest act of God's love that we will ever know. He is our High Priest and Savior. The blood of Jesus cleanses us from all of our sins. He is a part of the Godhead and always has been with the heavenly Father since *the beginning*. Jesus gave us the two greatest commandments: Love the Lord your God with all your heart, soul, mind, and strength, and love your neighbor as yourself. He teaches us to love our enemies and forgive those who have hurt us. Our Lord helps us to rediscover the original intent of the love of the Father and lets us know that we have choices to make every day of our lives that will affect our eternal destination. Jesus directs us to refocus our priorities in line with the kingdom of God. He told us the Father would welcome Gentiles as well as Jews into the kingdom, and then crossed cultural barriers to demonstrate the love of God to all mankind.

Love has found a way through Jesus Christ our Lord. The Father's love and plans for us have never changed, and Jesus came to set us on the right course. We will also discuss what love is and some of its characteristics as written in the thirteenth chapter of 1 Corinthians, the love chapter. Since God gave us a charge to love Him and to love others as ourselves, it is essential to know just what love consists of. This will be a self-examining chapter to help us align our concept of love with that of the heavenly Father.

The love of the Father continues as we discover how the Holy Spirit is the love of God in us. Love starts with the Father and is expressed and fulfilled by Jesus when He went to the cross and ascended to His throne in heaven. He then sent the Holy Spirit to guide and help us. The Holy Spirit is our helper and standby. He is in us to fulfill the will of the Father and Jesus in our lives and will help us to make the right decisions to have a more victorious life. It is up to us to be obedient and to make the right choices. We will also discuss the role of suffering in a Christian's life and why God allows us to suffer. Sometimes we bring on the suffering by our own bad choices while at other times we are attacked or become victims of circumstances or events that we do not have any control over.

Moving on in our journey of love, we discover how fear, the flesh, unforgiveness, and spiritual warfare bow their knee to the power of God's love in us. The Lord (Love) has given us a way to victory in our lives. We have to make the right choices and be ready to act upon the decisions we have made, yielding our will to that of the heavenly Father's will for us. This opens the door for the Holy Spirit to move in our lives and help us to complete the will of God in our lives.

To understand the love of the Father and see through His eyes will help us understand why we are here on this earth and what our purpose is. Some may feel that God has abandoned us in our pain and given us over to be devoured by this world. This book is written to remind us of God's original plan for mankind and each individual.

God's love for us has not failed. God's love for us is on a much higher level than we can comprehend. Some of us may have misunderstood what God's original plan for mankind was and the purpose and design of the Father's love toward each and every one of us. God's love for us and his plans for us are eternal, and yet the Father's love for us does not lose sight of our immediate needs and struggles. God's original plan is still the same—a loving relationship. We just need to understand more about the Father's love.

THE FATHER'S LOVE REVEALED IN CREATION

"*I*n the beginning God created the heavens and the earth. The earth was without form, and void; and darkness was on the face of the deep" (Genesis 1:1-2a, NKJ). Christian people within the body of Christ do disagree on some points of various doctrines of the Bible, but most agree with the verse given above in Genesis that God was the creator of the heavens and earth. It is not the intent or purpose of this book to discuss whether there was a lapse of time between verses 1 and 2 of this chapter. The focus of this book is to reveal the Father's love in His plan for mankind. Therefore, in referring to creation of the earth, I will use the word "Genesis" or creation/

restoration when applicable. Nevertheless, a plan was in motion to create a living being in God's own image that would execute dominion over the earth and, with his own free will, worship God his Creator in perfect fellowship. This was to be a labor of love.

The Word was with God at the time of creation/restoration. "In the beginning was the Word, and the Word was with God, and the Word was God. He was in the beginning with God. All things were made through Him, and without Him nothing was made that was made" (John 1:1-3, NKJ).

The Word is identified in verse 14 of this same chapter and reads as follows. "And the Word became flesh and dwelt among us, and we beheld His glory, the glory as of the only begotten of the Father, full of grace and truth" (John 1:14, NKJ). This scripture refers to Jesus, the Son of God. The Holy Spirit also had an active part of creation/restoration. "And the Spirit of God was hovering over the face of the waters" (Genesis 1:2b, NKJ). Let's take a closer look at this creation/restoration process and notice the care, love and perfection that went into making the earth.

> In the beginning God created the heavens and the earth. The earth was without form, and void; and darkness was on the face of the deep. And the Spirit of God was hovering over the face of the waters. Then God said, "Let there be light"; and there

was light. And God saw the light, that it
was good; and God divided the light from
the darkness. God called the light Day,
and the darkness He called Night. So the
evening and the morning were the first day.

—Genesis 1:1-5 (NKJ)

We can only imagine the scene as our heavenly
Father began to move upon the earth to bring
forth life as we know it. The world was covered in
darkness, and the earth was void, without form,
containing nothing—a wasteland. God called
forth light, separating the light from darkness,
making the morning and the evening the first
day. Try to imagine a world of darkness and void
of habitation, and then out of this chaos, there
comes light.

On the second day of Genesis, God made the
firmament (sky), and divided the waters from
under and above the sky. He then called the
firmament (sky) heaven.

Then God said, "Let there be a firmament
in the midst of the waters, and let it divide
the waters from the waters." Thus God
made the firmament, and divided the
waters which were under the firmament
from the waters which were above the
firmament; and it was so. And God called

the firmament Heaven. So the evening and
the morning were the second day.

—Genesis 1:6-8 (NKJ)

The earth was covered by water, and there would
have been a lot of vapor. As we will read in our next
scripture, the vapor (mist) went up and watered
the ground. God created the firmament to divide
these "waters" (the vapor and the water). This
was the beginning of a perfect weather system.
"For the Lord God had not caused it to rain on
the earth, and there was no man to till the ground;
but a mist went up from the earth and watered the
whole face of the ground" (Genesis 2:5b-6, NKJ).

As you can see, this is a well-thought-out plan.
God didn't just throw the planet together. The
purpose of this planet was for the habitation of
man to have authority over the earth and to be
responsible for its care. This was a work of love.
He built this world line upon line and precept
upon precept.

On the third day of Genesis:

> Then God said, "Let the waters under the
> heavens be gathered together in one place,
> and let the dry land appear"; and it was so.
> And God called the dry land Earth, and the
> gathering together of the waters He called
> Seas. And God saw that it was good. Then
> God said, "Let the earth bring forth grass,

the herb that yields seed, and the fruit tree that yields fruit according to its kind, whose seed is in itself, on the earth"; and it was so. And the earth brought forth grass, the herb that yields seed according to its kind, and the tree that yields fruit, whose seed is in itself according to its kind. And God saw that it was good. So the evening and the morning were the third day.

—Genesis 1:9-13 (NKJ)

Just think of it! This God of love called the waters and the land to their own boundaries. He then spoke forth all of the substance that was to be on the land. All of this came from the thoughts of God. He just spoke it forth. (I think I just made a big understatement.) Again, think of the precision and the order in which this was done.

On the fourth day of Genesis:

Then God said, "Let there be lights in the firmament of the heavens to divide the day from the night; and let them be for signs and seasons, and for days and years; and let them be for lights in the firmament of the heavens to give light on the earth"; and it was so. Then God made two great lights; the greater light to rule the day, and the lesser light to rule the night. He made the stars also. God set them in the firmament of the heavens to give light on the earth, and to rule over the day and over the night, and to divide the light from the darkness. And God saw that it was good. So the evening and the morning were the fourth day.

—Genesis 1:14-19 (NKJ)

God divided day and night and brought forth seasons, days and years. God made two great lights: a brighter light to rule the day (sun) and the lesser light to rule by night (moon). At this time He created / restored the stars. God set these lights in the heavens to give light on the earth. God has created the heavens and set them in place. Time itself was put in motion. All of this was done to create a positive effect and to help sustain the earth. God knew how to bring all of this into balance. The creation was not made by accident or by mistake. A God of great intelligence has done all of this for us. Is this not an act of great love?

So far God has made dry land and brought forth the trees and grass; He set boundaries for the waters and set the lights in the heavens. It is amazing to note the precision and order that God has taken in His creation. Consider the constellations. Have you ever just gazed at the stars on a clear night and marveled at the expansive beauty of the heavens? Did this all happen by accident? No other planet in our solar system is made like earth. Our planet is one of a kind. God created a world that was made to perfection—no hurricanes, windstorms, earthquakes, or tornadoes. The earth was like a beautiful garden without flaw. Only a God of love could make such a beautiful place. This world was not an accident that just happened.

On the fifth day of Genesis:

> Then God said, "Let the waters abound with an abundance of living creatures, and let birds fly above the earth across the face of the firmament of the heavens." So God created great sea creatures and every living thing that moves, with which the waters abounded, according to their kind, and every winged bird according to its kind. And God saw that it was good. And God blessed them, saying, "Be fruitful and multiply, and fill the waters in the seas, and let birds multiply on the earth." So the evening and the morning were the fifth day.
>
> —Genesis 1:20-23 (NKJ)

Winged birds were created to fly above the earth and the sea creatures and every living thing that moves in the waters. Have you ever visited an aquarium and were amazed at all the different kinds of life that exist? Scientists are still discovering new life in our oceans. Think of how birds were studied in order to figure out how man could fly with the invention of the airplane.

Have you ever marveled at how many kinds of birds there are? Their colors can be so bright and striking. It was God's idea first.

For the next day of creation/restoration, I will divide our scripture in two parts. The reason will be evident as we proceed. On the sixth day of Genesis:

> Then God said, "Let the earth bring forth the living creature according to its kind: cattle and creeping thing and beast of the earth, each according to its kind"; and it was so. And God made the beast of the earth according to its kind, cattle according to its kind, and everything that creeps on the earth according to its kind. And God saw that it was good.
>
> —Genesis 1:24-25 (NKJ)

All creatures that moved upon the face of the earth were made. For those of us who are animal lovers and have pets that we consider family members, this gift of creation is special. It is interesting to note that animals have their own distinct personality and habits that distinguish them from the rest of their kind. Animals, especially our domestic pets, give us unconditional love and comfort when needed. Of all of God's creation, our pets are a special gift of love from the heavenly Father, and I personally want to thank Him for it.

When I go to a zoo and see the big cats, I am awed by their magnificence as well as have a respect for their dependence or need for man. However, in the beginning, God created man and the animal kingdom to be compatible.

On the sixth day, God also created man, the most important and complex creation yet. God created the earth as a place of habitation for mankind.

> Then God said, "Let Us make man in Our image, according to Our likeness; Let them have dominion over the fish of the sea, over the birds of the air, and over the cattle, over all the earth and over every creeping thing that creeps on the earth." So God created man in His own image; in the image of God He created him; male and female He created them. Then God blessed them, and God said to them, "Be fruitful and multiply; fill the earth and subdue it; have dominion over the fish of the sea, over the birds of the air, and over every living thing that moves on the earth." And God said, "See, I have given you every herb that yields seed which is on the face of all the earth, and every tree whose fruit yields seed; to you it shall be for food. Also to every beast of the earth, to every bird of the air, and to everything that creeps on the earth, in which there is life, I have given every green herb for food"; and it was so. Then God saw everything that He

had made, and indeed it was very good. So the evening and the morning were the sixth day.

—Genesis 1:26-31 (NKJ)

Man was blessed and was told to be fruitful, multiply, and fill the earth. He was also told to subdue (to bring under control) the earth and have dominion (supreme control) over it. This included every living thing that moved on the earth, in the seas, and over the air. Every tree, herb, and fruit was given to man for food. God gave mankind the responsibility and authority of the earth and all that was in and over the earth. Some may wonder what He could have been thinking. Actually, this was no mistake on God's part. God doesn't make mistakes. He had a purpose in mind. God had faith and hope in the man that He had made. This is the action of a loving Father who wants good, responsible sons and daughters. I marvel at the authority that God gave mankind in giving him dominion (rule) over the earth.

The seventh day of Genesis was special. God was pleased with His creation and took a break. "And on the seventh day God ended His work which He had done, and He rested on the seventh day from all His work which He had done. Then God blessed the seventh day and sanctified it, because in it He rested from all His work which God had created and made" (Genesis 2:2-3, NKJ). This was a busy week for the Godhead. We can't begin to imagine the world in a perfect state. It must have been something that the word "beautiful" cannot even begin to describe.

God gave dominion and authority of the earth to Adam and his descendants. It would take some intelligence to assume this charge that God gave. Adam was made in God's image, and he was not a dumb ape-man. God does not create stupidity. If the world was created/restored in such perfection, why wouldn't man be created in perfection?

> Out of the ground the Lord God formed every beast of the field and every bird of the air, and brought them to Adam to see what he would call them. And whatever Adam called each living creature, that was its name. So Adam gave names to all cattle, to the birds of the air, and to every beast of the field. But for Adam there was not found a helper comparable to him.
>
> —Genesis 2:19-20 (NKJ)

We can't even begin to imagine the scope of this task, but Adam had supreme intelligence to carry out any assignment that God would have given him.

The reason that we have just taken a journey through the Genesis days is to understand the original plan and intent of the heavenly Father for mankind. God's intention for man was to live and have dominion in this perfect world that God had created and made for him. There was no sin, hurt, or pain at this time. Man was to have perfect fellowship with God and to live a perfect life in a perfect world. We need to understand that it is not God's fault that this world is messed up. So what went wrong? Now, the drama of the ages starts to unfold.

> Then the Lord God took the man and put him in the garden of Eden to tend and keep it. And the Lord God commanded the man, saying, "Of every tree of the garden you may freely eat; but of the tree of the knowledge of good and evil you shall not eat, for in the day that you eat of it you shall surely die."

> —Genesis 2:15-17 (NKJ)

This means that not only would his flesh die, but he would also experience spiritual death. The spirit in a man is eternal, but in spiritual death he will be separated from God. God did not make robots. Man was given a free will. Choices had to be made, independently of the Father's influence. God wants man, of his own free will, to love, worship, and obey him. This was a test to see what he would do. God gave Adam this command before Eve was created. The creation of Eve was one of a kind. The Lord made her from one of Adam's ribs.

> And the Lord God caused a deep sleep to fall on Adam, and he slept; and He took one of his ribs, and closed up the flesh in its place. Then the rib which the Lord God had taken from man He made into a woman, and He brought her to the man. And Adam said: "This is now bone of my bones and flesh of my flesh; she shall be called Woman, because she was taken out of Man." Therefore a man shall leave his father and mother and be joined to his wife, and they shall become one flesh."
>
> —Genesis 2:21-24 (NKJ)

Before continuing our story, let's do a little background on the next character—the villain—that came upon the scene. When we first read of this character, he was known as the serpent. "Now the serpent was more cunning than any beast of the field which the Lord God had made" (Genesis 3:1a, NKJ). This character is identified in the book of Revelation. "So the great dragon was cast out, that serpent of old, called the Devil and Satan, who deceives the whole world; he was cast to the earth, and his angels were cast out with him" (Revelation 12:9, NKJ). Obviously, the serpent was not good. He was called a deceiver, and he made trouble.

There are a couple of scriptures that would give you a little more insight and background into this villain's history. It is important that we know about this character of history especially because his influence and tactics remain to this day. In the following scriptures, God was speaking to Satan.

> You were in Eden, the garden of God; every precious stone was your covering: the sardius, topaz, and diamond, beryl, onyx, and jasper, sapphire, turquoise, and emerald with gold. The workmanship of your timbrels and pipes was prepared for you on the day you were created. You were the anointed cherub who covers; I established you; you were on the holy mountain of God; you walked back and forth in the midst of fiery stones. You were perfect in your ways from the day you were created, till iniquity was found in you.

—Ezekiel 28:13-15 (NKJ)

Satan was also created and had a top position in God's kingdom. Satan, who was first known as Lucifer, was an anointed cherub, an angel who was created in perfection. Angels, as well as men, have been given a free will and choices to make. Angels are also eternal beings. Lucifer made the wrong decisions and was rejected by God.

THE GREATEST OF THESE IS LOVE

How are you fallen from heaven, O Lucifer,
son of the morning! How you are cut down
to the ground, you who weakened the
nations! For you have said in your heart:
'I will ascend into heaven, I will exalt my
throne above the stars of God; I will also
sit on the mount of the congregation on
the farthest sides of the north; I will ascend
above the heights of the clouds, I will be
like the Most High.'

—Isaiah 14:12-14 (NKJ)

Lucifer committed treason against God. He was
blinded by pride. How could he, a created being
himself, think that he could be equal with God?
Lucifer lusted for power and worship. He wanted
to be like God and was jealous of Him. He was out
to destroy God's plans for mankind.

To continue our story, Adam and Eve were in
the Garden of Eden, and Satan, in the form of a
serpent, entered the scene. Remember at this point,
Satan was already a fallen creature and an enemy
of God.

Now the serpent was more cunning than
any beast of the field which the Lord God
had made. And he said to the woman, "Has
God indeed said, 'You shall not eat of every
tree of the garden'?" And the woman said
to the serpent, "We may eat the fruit of the

trees of the garden; but of the fruit of the tree which is in the midst of the garden, God has said, 'You shall not eat it, nor shall you touch it, lest you die.'" Then the serpent said to this woman, "You will not surely die. For God knows that in the day you eat of it your eyes will be opened, and you will be like God, knowing good and evil." So when the woman saw that the tree was good for food, that it was pleasant to the eyes, and a tree desirable to make one wise, she took of its fruit and ate. She also gave to her husband with her, and he ate. Then the eyes of both of them were opened, and they knew that they were naked; and they sewed fig leaves together and made themselves coverings.

—Genesis 3:1-7 (NKJ)

One day the serpent went to Eve to entice her to eat the fruit of the forbidden tree. He successfully deceived Eve and she ate of the fruit and then gave Adam some fruit, which he also ate. "And Adam was not deceived, but the woman being deceived, fell into transgression" (1 Timothy 2:14, NKJ). Their eyes were opened, and the damage was done. Of all that they had been given, they chose to eat the fruit of the forbidden tree. That was the only thing God had asked of them. Yes, God did put the tree in the garden because He wanted them to choose to obey and trust Him. It proved to be too tempting for Adam and Eve.

What followed is tragic and yet wondrous. God cursed the serpent in the first part of this verse, and then He spoke a prophecy over Satan, foretelling of his coming defeat on the earth.

> So the Lord God said to the serpent: "Because you have done this, you are cursed more than all cattle, and more than every beast of the field; on your belly you shall go, and you shall eat dust all the days of your life. And I will put enmity between you and the woman, and between your seed and her Seed; He shall bruise your head, and you shall bruise His heel."
>
> —Genesis 3:14-15 (NKJ)

Mankind was given a promise that the serpent will be defeated. The "Word" (Jesus) was to be born of a woman's seed, and He will crush the head of the serpent. It is mentioned that the serpent will bruise the heel of Jesus. The death, burial, and resurrection of Jesus seem more than a bruise, but look at the scope of the situation. Man was cut off from God. He was bound for spiritual death. The devil had taken the title deed of the earth from man, and the man had lost dominion over the earth. Right after the Lord cursed the serpent, the promise of the Messiah came forth. God had a backup plan, and it came at no small price. He would send His own Son to be a sacrifice for mankind and take on the penalty of sin for the redemption of their souls. It seems as though we are coming around full circle to what God intended—for us to make the right choices. "For God so loved the world that He gave His only begotten Son, that whoever believes in Him should not perish but have everlasting life" (John 3:16, NKJ).

I can only imagine the discussion of the Godhead as this plan was put into motion. The decision was enormous and unanimous. Jesus (the Word), the heavenly Father, and the Holy Spirit were, and always will be, in agreement. They are separate, and yet They are "one."

God could have just allowed us to get what we deserved—namely, an eternal spiritual death in serving the devil. Our Creator could have just destroyed us and started over. God's creation was on the brink of disaster; but God did not hesitate. Right after God cursed the serpent, the promise of the Messiah was pronounced. What love and sacrifice! It's hard to comprehend. In this most desperate hour, hope was given to the human race. God, Jesus, and the Holy Spirit looked beyond the cross and the pain. This was a plan that would bring eternal victory for God and would fulfill His original plan. He would have a family who would choose to love and worship Him of their own free will. Love cannot be commanded but must be freely given. Because of the knowledge of good and evil that Adam partook of, man now had to choose between good and evil. The earth was still cursed, but a plan was in motion to redeem man's eternal soul. This is probably the greatest evidence of the love of God that we will ever know. God gave His only Son as a sacrifice for us so that we can and will have life eternal with Him. Remember, God is looking at you through the eyes of eternity. The rest of this tragedy is predictable.

> Then the Lord God said, "Behold, the man has become like one of Us, to know good and evil. And now, lest he put out his hand and take also of the tree of life, and eat, and live forever—therefore the Lord God sent him out of the garden of Eden to till the ground from which he was taken. So He drove out the man; and He placed cherubim at the east of the garden of Eden, and a flaming sword which turned every way, to guard the way to the tree of life.
>
> —Genesis 3:22-24 (NKJ)

The perfection of the creation had fallen, and spiritual death began its work in the earth. God did not make this choice; man did. Death is still at work in the earth today, but those who believe in the sacrifice that Jesus has made are saved from the spiritual death that began in the Garden of

Eden. This is not what God wanted or intended for us.

In summary, we have been exploring the love of God in the creation/restoration story by examining the events day by day to see the love and care that God took in making a perfect world that man could live in. The world was not formed by accident. A supreme intelligence (God) spoke our earth into existence. The Father's original intent was to have the love, fellowship, and worship of man of his own free will. We were to be God's own extended family. The Creator's plans and intentions were all good for man. God only asked one thing of man, being that man would not eat of the fruit of the tree of the knowledge of good and evil. Man (Adam) chose to disobey, and that set in motion a chain of events that is occurring to this day. Sometimes we are quick to blame God for all the wrong in the earth. We need to put the blame on the right source.

The devil is at war with God to destroy all His plans for the earth and man. It is the devil that started the deception. Adam, who was a representative of mankind, chose to disobey God and eat of the fruit of the tree. Even after man did what he did, God did not give up on him. The promise of redemption was made at a great cost. This is the kind of love that we can hardly comprehend. This is the kind of love God has for each of us. "He who does not love does not know God, for God is love" (1 John 4:8, NKJ).

PERFECT LOVE
IN BALANCE

*I*n the previous chapter, we discovered God's original plan for man. He was not planning wars, famine, or sickness. This was not His intent. When man sinned, things changed. God's love for us did not change with the events that happened in the Garden of Eden.

We now need to discuss the other part of God's love and nature, which is holiness.

> Therefore gird up the loins of your mind, be sober, and rest your hope fully upon the grace that is to be brought to you at the revelation of Jesus Christ; as obedient children not conforming yourselves to the former lusts, as in your ignorance; but as He who called you is holy, you also be holy

in all your conduct, because it is written, "Be holy for I am holy."

—1 Peter 1:13-16 (NKJ)

Holiness is a part of God's love and nature. When we are living in holiness or righteousness, our conduct is in accordance with what is just or moral. "The righteous God wisely considers the house of the wicked, overthrowing the wicked for their wickedness" (Proverbs 21:12, NKJ). Just as light drives out darkness, God's light (holiness) drives out sin. Light and darkness cannot abide together. One will cancel out the other. Sin cannot remain in the presence of a holy God.

We must consider this factor when it comes to our heavenly Father and His dealings with His children. This is a big part of who God is. We want God to conform to our thinking and ways of doing things, but just the opposite is true. We need to renew our thinking and actions to His ways. We are not the source; God is. We don't make the rules; He does.

When sin entered into the earth through Adam, the earth was cursed, as was everything in it. Everything that God had made that was good was now impure. The blood sacrifice of animals was put in place to atone for the sins of man. This was a temporary measure until Jesus became the final blood sacrifice for us.

But Christ came as High Priest of the good things to come, with the greater and more perfect tabernacle not made with hands, that is, not of this creation. Not with the blood of goats and calves, but with His own blood He entered the Most Holy Place once for all, having obtained eternal redemption. For if the blood of bulls and goats and the ashes of a heifer, sprinkling the unclean, sanctifies for the purifying of the flesh, how much more shall the blood of Christ, who through the eternal Spirit offered Himself without spot to God, cleanse your conscience from dead works to serve the living God?

—Hebrews 9:11-14 (NKJ)

This was grace magnified toward us. Jesus was indeed the greatest gift of love from the heavenly Father; therefore, we cannot take this great love lightly. Jesus redeemed us from the curse of the law. We do not have to do daily offerings or blood sacrifices. We do not have to constantly wash and cleanse to keep from being impure.

The next time you read Exodus and Leviticus in the Bible, stop and think of all those laws and rules the people had to adhere to in order to be able to come before God. There were many grain and animal sacrifices that had to be fulfilled. In some cases, especially for the priests that ministered before the Lord on behalf of the people, death could occur if certain duties were not fulfilled in a certain way. Jesus did not do away with the law, but He fulfilled it. Jesus is speaking in the following verse. "Do not think that I came to destroy the Law or the Prophets. I did not come to destroy but to fulfill" (Matthew 5:17, NKJ). We are currently in the age of grace.

This does not mean that God has changed His mind concerning sin. He has not changed personalities from the Old to the New Testament in the Bible. Love and holiness are part of who He is; they are part of His nature. It is critical to understand this in trying to comprehend the love of God and the Godhead in their dealings with the nations, church, and individuals. This love and holiness come together in perfect balance. The world and its thinking, technology, and degenerating morals are in constant change, but God has not changed His thinking or His methods in dealing with His children or with the world.

He still loves man. He proved it by sending Jesus into the world. He still hates sin and evil and will not tolerate it among His people. This is who He is, and He will win in the end. We read this in the book of Revelation. Jesus will come back and form a government here on earth; it will be a kingdom, not a democracy or a global government. The earth will have one king, and that king will be Jesus Christ.

We are not going to be able to bring God down to our level, but He will bring us up to His level. All those who believe and obey his commands, as children should obey a father who loves them, will reign with Jesus in this new world kingdom. "Then the seventh angel sounded: And there were loud voices in heaven, saying, 'The kingdoms of this world have become the kingdoms of our Lord and of His Christ, and He shall reign forever and ever!'" (Revelation 11:15, NKJ). Every time you pray the Lord's Prayer, you are praying for His kingdom to come on this earth. "Your kingdom come. Your will be done on earth as it is in heaven" (Luke 11:2b, NKJ).

If a loving earthly father sees his children going down a destructive path or finds them in disobedience, discipline is in order. I want to stress here that God is not a child abuser. There are many fathers in the world who are abusers and use discipline that is not mixed with love to teach their children "a lesson." These measures will end in children who are rebellious or children who become "victims." Discipline is also a part of love. It is called "tough love." It doesn't feel good to the flesh and can be temporarily painful.

Punishment can be given out in love or anger. When God disciplines one of His children or even when He disciplines a nation, it is always in love, because that is who He is. "You should know in your heart that as a man chastens his son, so the Lord your God chastens you" (Deuteronomy 8:5,

NKJ). God treats His children the same way. If we get out of line, we will be disciplined. His holiness, righteousness, and love are in perfect balance. The following is an example of the Father's love in action where we can see these two natures (love and holiness) at work.

King David's story is probably one of the most familiar in the Old Testament. David loved the Lord and kept His commandments. The Lord gave him the authority to reign over Israel. This was a great honor and David was handpicked and anointed by God. With great power comes great responsibility—and consequences. When King David made a mistake, the Lord did not overlook the situation.

Let's pick up the story after David committed adultery with Bathsheba, and she became pregnant. David had Uriah, Bathsheba's husband, brought back from the battlefield in order to be with his wife, therefore concealing David's sin. However, because of his dedication to the armies of Israel and his king, Uriah did not use the privilege to go to his house or see his wife, but slept at the door of the king's house. David then had Uriah murdered on the front lines of battle so that Bathsheba could become his wife. The Lord then sent Nathan, a prophet, to confront David. Nathan didn't start out blaming and condemning David but presented to him a situation to help David realize what he had done.

Then the Lord sent Nathan to David. And he came to him, and said to him: "There were two men in one city, the one rich and the other poor. The rich man had exceedingly many flocks and herds. But the poor man had nothing except one little ewe lamb which he had bought and nourished; and it grew up together with him and with his children. It ate of his own food and drank from his own cup and lay in his bosom; and it was like a daughter to him. And a traveler came to the rich man, who refused to take from his own flock and from his own herd to prepare one for the wayfaring man who had come to him; but he took the poor man's lamb and prepared it for the man who had come to him." So David's anger was greatly aroused against the man, and he said to Nathan, "As the Lord lives, the man who has done this shall surely die! And he shall restore fourfold for the lamb, because he did this thing and because he had no pity." Then Nathan said to David, "You are the man! Thus says the Lord God of Israel: 'I anointed you king over Israel, and I delivered you from the hand of Saul. I gave your master's house and your master's wives into your keeping, and gave you the house of Israel and Judah. And if that had been too little, I also would have given you much more! Why have you despised the commandment of the Lord, to do evil in His sight? You have killed Uriah the Hittite with the sword; you have taken his wife to be your wife, and have killed him with the sword of the people of Ammon. Now therefore, the sword shall never depart from your house, because you have despised Me, and have taken the wife of Uriah the Hittite to be your wife.' "Thus says the Lord, 'Behold, I will raise up adversity against you from your own house; and I will take your wives before your eyes and give them to your neighbor, and he shall lie with your wives in the sight of this sun. For you did it secretly, but I will do this thing before all Israel, before the sun.'" So David said to Nathan, "I have sinned against the Lord." And Nathan said to David, "The Lord also has put away your sin; you shall not die. However, because by this deed you have given great occasion to the enemies of the Lord to blaspheme, the child also who is born to you shall surely die." Then Nathan departed to his house.

—2 Samuel 12:1-15 (NKJ)

In these verses you can see the love and the discipline (holiness and righteousness) of God. Nathan told David a story that coincided with David's situation. This was done to get David to look at the situation from the position of a king rather than just a man with lust and murder in his heart. When David looked at the situation from a king's standpoint, not realizing it was himself who was in question, he was ready to put the culprit to death as well as make restitution. Nathan then revealed that David was the guilty one.

The Lord spoke through Nathan and reminded David of all that He had given him in making him King of Israel and protecting him from Saul. The Lord mentions that He would have given David even more things if he wanted. This is a God who wants to bless his children and care for those that love and obey him. One can almost feel the pain that the Lord is feeling as He asks David, if in disobeying His commandment by committing adultery and murder was how he was repaying God for His goodness to him.

The Lord even mentions that in breaking the commandment of the Lord, David has despised Him. God takes this personally. Imagine the conflict inside of a loving parent who has to discipline his child for disobedience. The two natures are in conflict. There is a desire to show mercy and love and the need to see that the right action is taken for the child's sake because of the consequences that might happen to the child if he is not corrected. The child, (in this case, King David) could continue on the wrong path, believing he can get away with disobedience (sin).

King David's actions also affected other people. A man was murdered, and a wife was made a widow. David was a king, and a nation of people knew him as a servant of God. Our loving heavenly Father could not, and would not, overlook this situation. It was with deep sorrow that the Lord pronounced judgment upon David. Violence (the sword) would continue in David's family. His wives would be taken from him. As David tried to hide his sin, the Lord was going to make an open book of all that had happened to all of Israel. The secret was not going to be a secret anymore. Can you imagine the gossip and scandal this caused in Jerusalem and throughout all of Israel? People would talk of that sordid tale for a long time. It did not please God to do this, and it was not of His choosing. David chose to sin, and he was responsible for that sin.

Again, I say, God will not let sin stand in His presence. He is holy, He is righteous, and He is love. In just one verse David repents, and he is forgiven. God is always ready to forgive. This doesn't mean that there aren't consequences to pay when we do wrong.

The Lord makes an interesting statement to the fact that David has given occasion to the enemies of the Lord to blaspheme. David opened the door for the enemy to come in and slander God because of his (David's) actions. Let's not forget the devil is still at work in the earth. Once the door is opened by our sin, the devil will not fail to walk in and use every opportunity to his advantage for the kingdom of darkness.

Among his people, David was known for his love for God. In today's world, when a righteous person (such as a pastor) commits sin and falls from grace, it gives people the opportunity to not only blame the person but blame and speak evil of God. Before you know it, all people who love God and are righteous are depicted as hypocrites and phonies, as well. God wants us to be lights in the world and not be a part of the darkness. We are the living examples of Christ who stand in the earth as David was an example before his people of the heavenly Father. To whom much has been given, much is required. We are responsible for the light we have, just as David was.

If we were to continue on with our story of David, we would find out that every word of the prophecy that Nathan spoke over David came true. As we can see in David's case, the price was great because his son died. Even in this tragedy, David had hope. After fasting to no avail for his son, he made a statement later on in this same chapter:

> And he said, 'While the child was alive, I fasted and wept; for I said, "Who can tell whether the Lord will be gracious to me, that the child may live?" But now he is dead; why should I fast? Can I bring him

back again? I shall go to him, but he shall not return to me.'"

—2 Samuel 12:22-23 (NKJ)

David could have been bitter or angry, but he chose to believe the God he loved; and he did so with his whole heart and was able to find peace not only in the forgiveness that God had given him, but also in the judgment.

This is not to say that for anyone who commits adultery and murder; their child will die. Remember that David knew and experienced much of the grace and goodness of the Lord. David saw and experienced the miracles of God. He also knew not to sin. God deals with us on an individual basis, as only He can know our heart. He is the righteous judge. Remember, to those whom have been given much, much is required. "But he who did not know, yet committed things deserving of stripes, shall be beaten with few. For everyone to whom much is given, from him much will be required; and to whom much has been committed, of him they will ask the more" (Luke 12:48, NKJ).

In summary, God has two natures in dealing with the world, the church, and His children as individuals. He is holy and righteous, and yet He is kind, merciful, and loving. The ingredient that puts this all together is love—because God *is* love. In God, love and holiness are in perfect balance.

We as God's creation have choices to make every day of what is right and what is wrong. We are responsible for the choices we make. There can be consequences if we are disobedient or make the wrong choices. God is not abusive. He does not take pleasure in seeing us in pain. This was not His intention even from the beginning of creation, but because He is a holy God, He will discipline us when we do wrong just as any good father would. We often think of God's love on our level and our terms. God wants to bring us up to His level, and this is the whole point in regards to God and His dealing with His creation. His ways are better than our ways, and His thoughts are better than our thoughts. Sometimes it is hard to comprehend or to understand this love. This is where trust comes in. "The Lord redeems the soul of His servants, and none of those who trust in Him shall be condemned" (Psalm 34:22, NKJ).

THE FATHER'S LOVE IN THE OLD TESTAMENT

*I*t took me a long time to understand that God showed people love in the Old Testament. I thought judgment and God's anger was all that was offered to the poor souls back in that time. It just seemed as if God was always mad at everyone. I was very wrong. God's love has always been and will be consistent.

What throws us off is the fact that man operated under the Law of Moses at the time. Now we live under grace because the blood of Jesus has blotted out our sin. Animal sacrifice was accepted by God as a covering for sin, but this was only a temporary measure. The Law of Moses served as a demonstration of God's love because these laws served as a link to God. Otherwise we would be separated from God because we could not come to Him in our sinful condition.

Too many times we take the holiness of God too lightly. God's love for us is unconditional, and that will never change. However, because of the fall of man in the Garden of Eden, the earth was cursed and so was man. The blessings of God are conditional. Salvation is free. In the Old Testament, obedience to God's laws was crucial. God is a holy God, and sin cannot be in His presence, yet He wanted to be with His children.

This brings mankind to the place where he has to make life choices. If we choose to obey and love God, the blessings of God will be ours. If we choose to live our lives without God, we are in disobedience, and consequences could follow. This doesn't always result in death and destruction, but please realize that when we make the wrong choices, we are leaving the door wide open for the devil to walk in and bring a lot of misery with him. The devil hates mankind and would like nothing better than to destroy God's most wondrous creation.

In Deuteronomy 28 we can find the blessings of obedience and the curses of disobedience. Now, you may ask, how could Deuteronomy 28, in any way, describe the love of God? It sounds more like a threat than love speaking. However, what more could a loving father do with his child other than communicate the right things to do to succeed in life and the rewards that will be reaped?

A wise father will also warn the child of what will happen when the wrong choices are made and of the trouble and danger that could follow. Parents who care about their children will warn them against drugs, the dangers of smoking, riotous living, and forming friendships with people of bad influence. These are just a few of the things that need to be discussed to help teach the child to make the right decisions.

It is no different with God. Our heavenly Father wants His children to succeed and make the right choices so that life will go well for them. Our God has even more of a right to give us these guidelines and directions because the choices we make for Him are eternal, and the consequences of our choices, good or bad, will last forever. Now in Deuteronomy 28, God is speaking to Israel as a nation as well as individuals. We are going to look at the verses of scripture that contain the blessings of being obedient to God and then the verses of scripture that contain the curses that come upon us when we choose to be disobedient. In this reading we can get a clear picture of a loving Father giving His children instruction and the results of choosing to serve Him or not to serve Him. The following scripture is about the blessings upon the obedient.

> Now it shall come to pass, if you diligently obey the voice of the Lord your God, to observe carefully all His commandments which I command you today, that the Lord

your God will set you high above all the
nations of the earth. And all these blessings
shall come upon you and overtake you,
because you obey the voice of the Lord
your God: Blessed shall you be in the city,
and blessed shall you be in the country.
Blessed shall be the fruit of your body, the
produce of your ground and the increase
of your herds, the increase of your cattle
and the offspring of your flocks. Blessed
shall be your basket and your kneading
bowl. Blessed shall you be when you come
in, and blessed shall you be when you go
out. The Lord will cause your enemies who
rise against you to be defeated before your
face; they shall come out against you one
way and flee before you seven ways. The
Lord will command the blessing on you in
your storehouses and in all to which you
set your hand, and He will bless you in the
land which the Lord your God is giving
you. The Lord will establish you as a holy
people to Himself, just as He has sworn to
you, if you keep the commandments of the
Lord your God and walk in His ways. Then
all peoples of the earth shall see that you
are called by the name of the Lord, and they
shall be afraid of you.

—Deuteronomy 28:1-10 (NKJ)

Remember whom God is talking to. These are His chosen people who said they would forsake all gods and follow after Him. They were operating under the Law of Moses. Even though there was a different covenant in place for them, the blessings and curses still apply to His children today under the covenant that Jesus established for us. If we choose to follow God and obey His commandments, we will be blessed.

Look at America. We can definitely see that God has blessed America since it was founded on godly principles. America is one of the most prosperous and blessed countries on this planet. This writing is not meant for any political or national views, but I believe this is a true statement, and the Lord is pleased that we acknowledge the truth. God wants to see His children blessed.

In these scriptures, the Lord says that we will prosper, and anywhere we go we will flourish. We are blessed with material possessions. Our children are blessed, and all that we have. The Lord will defeat our enemies before us, and He will make us a part of His family. To obey Him and keep His commandments is the condition for these blessings. Make the right choices, and you will be blessed. This doesn't mean that trials of life won't happen. Life happens, and all that goes with it. Remember, Adam ate the fruit of the tree, which brought the curse upon the earth, but God's intention is to bless you and help you through the trials of life. It is now time to look at the scriptures that describe the curses that come upon the disobedient.

> But it shall come to pass, if you do not obey the voice of the Lord your God, to observe carefully all His commandments and His statutes which I command you today, that all these curses will come upon you and overtake you: Cursed shall you be in the city, and cursed shall you be in the country. Cursed shall be your basket and your kneading bowl. Cursed shall be the fruit of your body and the produce of your land, the increase of your cattle and the offspring of your flocks. Cursed shall you be when you come in, and cursed shall you be when you go out. The Lord will send on you cursing, confusion, and rebuke in all that you set your hand to do, until you are destroyed and until you perish quickly, because of the wickedness of your doings in which you have forsaken Me. The Lord will make the plague cling to you until He has consumed you from the land which you are going to possess. The Lord will strike you with consumption, with fever, with inflammation, with severe burning fever, with the sword, with scorching, and with mildew; they shall pursue you until you perish. And your heavens which are over your head shall be bronze, and the earth

GLENDA HAINES

which is under you shall be iron. The Lord
will change the rain of your land to powder
and dust; from the heaven it shall come
down on you until you are destroyed. The
Lord will cause you to be defeated before
your enemies; you shall go out one way
against them and flee seven ways before
them; and you shall become troublesome
to all the kingdoms of the earth.

—Deuteronomy 28:15-25 (NKJ)

The Lord is saying just the opposite of what he
said in the blessings for being obedient. It is self-
explanatory. Is God being a hard taskmaster here?

Remember God is love. Love is not just an
adjective that describes God. Love is who and
what He is. There is no real love without Him. God
is all that is right and good and pleasant in this
world. The opposite of good is evil. The opposite
of love is hate. There is no middle ground. To
"ride the fence" and not make a choice is the
wrong choice. "I know your works, that you are
neither cold nor hot. I could wish you were cold
or hot. So then, because you are lukewarm, and
neither cold nor hot, I will vomit you out of My
mouth" (Revelation 3:15-16, NKJ). If we choose to
disobey God and not walk in His commandments,
the curse will come upon us. To not choose love
(God), is to automatically choose hate whether we
are aware of it or not.

Every day we choose life or death in the way we treat God and the way we treat others. God wants us to choose life and live with Him forever in a glory of perfection that we can't even imagine. Choices are what our life on earth is about. Our eternal life is a product of the choices we make today and every day.

The Old Testament is not a history of the world. It is a history of the genealogy of Jesus Christ, the Messiah. In preparing to bring Jesus to the earth, the Lord chose a man called Abraham and made a promise to him.

> Now the Lord had said to Abram: "Get out of your country, from your family and from your father's house, to a land that I will show you. I will make you a great nation; I will bless you and make your name great; and you shall be a blessing. I will bless those who bless you, and I will curse him who curses you; and in you all the families of the earth shall be blessed.
>
> —Genesis 12:1-3 (NKJ)

Abraham had a son called Isaac, and then Isaac had a son called Jacob. "And God said to him, 'Your name is Jacob; your name shall not be called Jacob anymore, but Israel shall be your name.' So He called his name Israel" (Genesis 35:10, NKJ). This is also the name of the great nation that God promised to Abraham. Jesus Christ was born in Israel, and He was a Jew. Through this nation of Israel, all the families of the earth have been blessed. The salvation that we have, even our faith, has Jewish roots. The devil wanted to wipe out the Jewish people, but God used miracles and whatever it took to insure that the plan of salvation would come to the earth. Think of the miracle of the children of Israel at the Red Sea. God parted the waters, so that they could pass by on dry ground.

> But the children of Israel had walked on dry land in the midst of the sea, and the waters were a wall to them on their right hand and on their left. So the Lord saved Israel that day out of the hand of the Egyptians, and Israel saw the Egyptians dead on the seashore.
>
> —Exodus 14:29-30 (NKJ)

Miracles were an everyday sight for these people. They were fed supernaturally, and every need was taken care of during their journey to claim the land that God gave them. When they disobeyed, they were disciplined. The blessings of God are not to be taken lightly. The children of Israel witnessed many great miracles of God and therefore they had a great responsibility to obey God's commands and follow Him. Our heavenly Father supernaturally protected them from armies that were stronger than they were. I can't imagine the love and patience it took for God to persevere all the times the people strayed and refused to serve Him. At all times there seemed to be at least one whom God would find to serve Him. So much was at stake! God never gave up. It took thousands of years before the time was right for the Messiah to come. Our heavenly Father must have experienced much agony over the choices of man, and yet love prevailed.

One of my favorite encounters of God's love for His people is while they were traveling in the wilderness on the way to the land that God had promised them. The story of Balak and Balaam is recorded in the book of Numbers 22-24. Let's do the condensed version so we can draw out the main points and keep on the target of showing forth God's love.

The children of Israel were camped on the plains of Moab. Balak was the king of Moab and afraid of the people of Israel because of their numbers. He decided to call for Balaam, a prophet from Mesopotamia, to curse the people. The Lord tells Balaam not to go with the messengers that Balak had sent. "And God said to Balaam, 'You shall not go with them; you shall not curse the people, for they are blessed'" (Numbers 22:12, NKJ). Balaam relayed the message to the messengers, but they persisted and persuaded Balaam to change his mind. They offered him all kinds of wealth. Balaam was flattered and offered to go to the

Lord for the second time to see if God would have anything else to say. The second time that Balaam approached God, he was given permission to go with the messengers; however, God was not pleased with Balaam.

The next morning Balaam saddled his donkey and headed out with his visitors. On the pathway, the Angel of the Lord was standing with his sword drawn to strike down Balaam. The donkey could see the angel, but Balaam could not. Three times the donkey tried to avoid the angel, and each time Balaam (who could not see the angel) struck the donkey. Let's see what happens next.

> Then the Lord opened the mouth of the donkey, and she said to Balaam, "What have I done to you, that you have struck me these three times?" And Balaam said to the donkey, "Because you have abused me. I wish there were a sword in my hand, for now I would kill you!" So the donkey said to Balaam, "Am I not your donkey on which you have ridden, ever since I became yours, to this day? Was I ever disposed to do this to you?" And He said, "No." Then the Lord opened Balaam's eyes, and he saw the Angel of the Lord standing in the way with His drawn sword in His hand; and he bowed his head and fell flat on his face. And the Angel of the Lord said to him, "Why

have you struck your donkey these three times? Behold, I have come out to stand against you, because your way is perverse before Me. The donkey saw Me and turned aside from Me these three times. If she had not turned aside from Me, surely I would also have killed you by now, and let her live."

—Numbers 22:28-33 (NKJ)

And people say that dogs are loyal! When I read this scripture, I am always surprised that there is no dialogue about the fact that a donkey is speaking to his master in an understandable voice. This could be the first Dr. Doolittle on record. I am surprised that Balaam didn't pass out from shock.

More important, what was happening here? Something was wrong within the heart of Balaam. He was much too eager to please the Moabites. God saw his heart. We must be careful of the choices we make. (Is this beginning to sound familiar?) Balaam repents, and the Angel of the Lord tells him to continue with the men but to only speak the words that he is given.

In chapter 23, Balak has taken Balaam to the high places of Baal to make burnt offerings to the Lord so that the people of Israel will be cursed. Balaam then spoke not a curse but a blessing over Israel. This made Balak furious. So he took Balaam to another place, and another offering was sent up. The same thing happened. Instead of cursing Israel, Balaam blessed Israel. "God is not a man, that He should lie, nor a son of man, that He should repent. Has he said, and will he not do? Or has He spoken and will He not make it good? Behold, I have received a command to bless; He has blessed, and I cannot reverse it" (Numbers 23:20, NKJ). Again the third time, Balak took Balaam to a different place to overlook the camp of Israel. For the third time, Balaam spoke blessings over Israel.

After this, each of the parties went their own way. In the following scripture, the heart of Balaam is unveiled. "Now when Balaam saw that it pleased the Lord to bless Israel, he did not go as at other times, to seek to use sorcery, but he set his face toward the wilderness" (Numbers 24:1, NKJ). Here it is revealed that Balaam did, at times, use sorcery. This was definitely against the laws of God.

> There shall not be found among you anyone who makes his son or his daughter pass through the fire, or one who practices witchcraft, or a soothsayer, or one who interprets omens, or a sorcerer, or one who conjures spells, or a medium, or a spiritist, or one who calls up the dead. For all who do these things are an abomination to the Lord, and because of these abominations

the Lord your God drives them out from
before you.

—Deuteronomy 18:10-12 (NKJ)

The Lord was using Balaam just as he used Pharaoh
in delivering the people out of Egypt. Balaam was
used to bless instead of curse God's people. The
moral of this story is that you cannot curse what
God has blessed.

In this next scripture, Moses is talking to the
people of Israel concerning those to be excluded
from the congregation of Israel.

> An Ammonite or a Moabite shall not enter
> the assembly of the Lord; even to the tenth
> generation none of his descendants shall
> enter the assembly of the Lord forever,
> because they did not meet you with bread
> and water on the road when you came out
> of Egypt, and because they hired against
> you Balaam the son of Beor from Pethor of
> Mesopotamia, to curse you. Nevertheless
> the lord your God would not listen to
> Balaam, but the Lord your God turned the
> curse into a blessing for you, because the
> Lord your God loves you.

—Deuteronomy 23:3-5 (NKJ)

God turned the curse into a blessing for them because He loved them. The people of Moab hired Balaam to curse Israel. They chose not to bless Israel. Therefore, God did not allow them into the assembly (congregation) of the Lord. God took this personally. In this next scripture, King David offers thanksgiving for His care and protection that was given to the children of Israel as they journeyed in the wilderness. "When they went from one nation to another, and from one kingdom to another people, He permitted no man to do them wrong; yes, He rebuked kings for their sakes, saying, 'Do not touch My anointed ones, and do My prophets no harm'" (1Chronicles 16:20-22, NKJ).

It can be a dangerous thing to mess with God's people. What happened to Balaam? "The children of Israel also killed with the sword Balaam the son of Beor, the soothsayer, among those who were killed by them" (Joshua 13:22, NKJ). To strike out at God's people is to strike out at God. The children of Israel did not have easy times. There were many hardships and weary days. They worked hard and were constantly traveling. They had to fight many battles in order to inherit their land. But one thing is for sure. God loved, guided, and protected them the whole way, and He is still doing it to this day, for any nation or individual who will call upon Him.

The story of Hosea and Gomer is one more example out of the Old Testament that demonstrates the love of God. The setting is a time of prosperity for Israel. An immoral lifestyle was in abundance as well as hatred. Prejudices abounded among the social classes. Corruption was in the leadership of Israel, and the basic family life was unstable. Political collapse of the nation was inevitable.

God invented a very different way of showing the people of Israel His love. This would be by having Hosea, a prophet of God, marry a prostitute, whose name was Gomer. Hosea was to be a living demonstration of God's love. Hosea represented God and the love He had for Israel. Gomer, an impure woman who was bound to stray and betray, represented the nation of Israel.

The Lord is speaking to Hosea in the following scripture. "Go, take yourself a wife of harlotry and children of harlotry, for the land has committed great harlotry by departing from the Lord" (Hosea 1:2b, NKJ). Here is where we began to see the judgment and the mercy of God working side by side as we have discussed in the previous chapter. Gomer bears Hosea three children.

> So he went and took Gomer the daughter of Diblaim, and she conceived and bore him a son. Then the Lord said to him: "Call his name Jezreel, for in a little while I will avenge the bloodshed of Jezreel on the house of Jehu, and bring an end of the kingdom of the house of Israel. It shall come to pass in that day that I will break the bow of Israel in the Valley of Jezreel." And she conceived

again and bore a daughter. Then God said to him: "Call her name Lo-Ruhamah, for I will no longer have mercy on the house of Israel, but I will utterly take them away. Yet I will have mercy on the house of Judah, will save them by the Lord their God, and will not save them by bow, nor by sword or battle, by horses or horsemen." Now, when she had weaned Lo-Ruhamah, she conceived and bore a son. Then God said: "Call his name Lo-Ammi, for you are not My people, and I will not be your God.

—Hosea 1:3-9 (NKJ)

You can just almost sense the anger and fire in God's eyes as well as feel the hurt in His heart. God was lamenting over his people, and there was pain involved for Him. He was like a rejected lover. However, no sooner does God pronounce judgment than grace appears. This is who He is—a God of holiness and mercy. He is a God of judgment because of His holiness and a God of mercy because of His love. Our heavenly Father is still speaking of His people in the following scripture.

Yet the number of the children of Israel shall be as the sand of the sea, which cannot be measured or numbered. And it shall come to pass in the place where it was said to them, "You are not My people," there it shall be said to them "you are sons of the living God." Then the children of Judah and the children of Israel shall be gathered together, and appoint for themselves one head; and they shall come up out of the land, for great will be the day of Jezreel!

—Hosea 1:10-11 (NKJ)

In these scriptures our Lord is promising the people that He will draw them back to Himself and bring them together as a nation again. At this time in Israel's history, Israel was divided into two nations: Judah and Israel.

In chapter two of Hosea, God is reminding His people of the unfaithfulness to Him. Just as Hosea struggles with his relationship with Gomer, God struggles with His relationship with the people of Israel.

Bring charges against your mother, bring charges; for she is not My wife, nor am I her Husband! Let her put away her harlotries from her sight, and her adulteries from between her breasts; lest I strip her naked and expose her, as in the day she was born, and make her like a wilderness, and set her like a dry land, and slay her with thirst.

—Hosea 2:2-3 (NKJ)

In chapter two of Hosea, the jealousy and pain of the Lord begins to give way to His mercy. "I will betroth you to Me forever; yes, I will betroth you to Me in righteousness and justice, in loving kindness and mercy; I will betroth you to Me in faithfulness, and you shall know the Lord" (Hosea 2:19-20, NKJ).

In chapter three of Hosea, Gomer has apparently left Hosea and gone back to her old lifestyle of prostitution. God tells him to go get her back. In these scriptures you can see the actual comparison God is making between Hosea/Gomer and God/Israel.

> Then the Lord said to me, "Go again, love a woman who is loved by a lover and is committing adultery, just like the love of the Lord for the children of Israel, who look to other gods and love the raisin cakes of the pagans." So I bought her for myself for fifteen shekels of silver, and one and one-half homers of barley. And I said to her, "You shall stay with me many days; you shall not play the harlot, nor shall you have a man—so, too, will I be toward you." For the children of Israel shall abide many days without king or prince, without sacrifice or sacred pillar, without ephod or teraphim. Afterward the children of Israel shall return and seek the Lord their God and David

their king. They shall fear the Lord and His goodness in the latter days."

—Hosea 3:1-5 (NKJ)

In this day and age, adultery and betrayal are too often the norm. The pain is no different now than it was back then and no different for us than for God. Sometimes we think of God as an "entity out there somewhere" that has no feelings. Our heavenly Father is the one who made us in His image. God has emotions. He can be jealous, angry, sad, and glad, and He is even known to laugh. "He who sits in the heavens shall laugh" (Psalm 2:4a, NKJ). In the book of Hosea, God was feeling betrayed just like a man who has an unfaithful wife. The message is that even though she was unfaithful, she was still loved and sought out to be brought back by her husband and to be loved in the right environment where there is safety and an enduring relationship. It is also the way God feels about us today as His people collectively as well as individuals. He is a God of love. It affects Him when we ignore or disobey Him. God is not a man; therefore, His love has endured a lot more of our rebellion than we could ever imagine. The heavenly Father is just not an object that we can ignore with our unfaithfulness. Sometimes our hearts are too hardened to hear the "Lover of our soul" speak to us.

In summary, we have looked at a few situations in which God has demonstrated His love in the Old Testament for His people. In the story of Balaam and Balack, we found that you cannot curse what God has blessed, and God is able to turn a curse into a blessing. Balaam paid, with his life, the price for his wicked heart and for his willingness to curse Israel. The constancy is still there. God is holy and righteous, and He is also merciful and loving. When we disobey, there can be discipline in store for us as it was for the children of Israel. God's will is to show mercy and to have His children be with him. It all comes down to choices.

Just to look at God's dealings with the children of Israel in the wilderness on their way to the "Promised Land" is a great example of our Father's love. He miraculously fed them, parted the Red Sea, led them by a pillar of fire at night and a cloud by day, and healed them, just to mention a few things. The children of Israel saw the miracles of God every day.

Hosea and Gomer were a demonstration of God's love in action. At God's instruction, Hosea married Gomer, a prostitute, to demonstrate the love of God toward His people. Our Father's children were in great rebellion, and He wanted to let them know that judgment was coming; however, salvation and restoration would also come. Even though He despised their sin, He wanted to forgive them and bring them back to Him.

JESUS: OUR EXAMPLE OF LOVE

*J*esus is a part of the Godhead. He was with the Father in the beginning of creation. Jesus spent a lot of time with the religious leaders of the day to discuss who He was, where He was from, what His teachings were about, and most importantly, that the Father had sent Him. Jesus reveals the Father to us. "Phillip said to Him, 'Lord, show us the Father, and it is sufficient for us.' Jesus said to him, 'Have I been with you so long, and yet you have not known Me, Phillip? He who has seen Me has seen the Father; so how can you say, "Show us the Father"?'" (John 14:8-9, NKJ).

Phillip was one of the disciples of Jesus and was with Him every day for about three years, and it was hard for him to understand the relationship of Jesus and the Father. At that time most of the disciples did not understand the mission that

Jesus had in coming to the earth. They were thinking Jesus would set up an earthly kingdom and deliver them from the Roman Empire that held them captive. If His own disciples could not comprehend what Jesus was saying, the religious leaders really had a problem. They thought He was a troublemaker who would cause a rebellion and make trouble with the Romans. The religious leaders saw Jesus as a threat to their faith and nation. Of course, I am sure that jealousy played a big part in the communication gap. In the following scripture, Jesus had just healed a man on the Sabbath. This made the Jews very angry because, by their religious law, no physical work was to be done on the Sabbath.

> Therefore the Jews sought all the more to kill Him, because He not only broke the Sabbath, but also said that God was His Father, making Himself equal with God. Then Jesus answered and said to them, "Most assuredly, I say to you the Son can do nothing of Himself, but what He sees the Father do; for whatever He does, the Son also does in like manner. For the Father loves the Son, and shows Him all things that He Himself does; and He will show Him greater works than these, that you may marvel. For as the Father raises the dead and gives life to them, even so the Son gives life to whom He will. For the

> Father judges no one, but has committed all
> judgment to the Son, that all should honor
> the Son just as they honor the Father. He
> who does not honor the Son does not honor
> the Father who sent Him.

—John 5:18-23 (NKJ)

As Jesus is the Son of God, the love of the Father is definitely in Jesus. Who better is qualified to show us the right way to live and love? As a man, Jesus could understand man's temptations and trials in life. As a perfect man, having overcome all temptations, He is the perfect High Priest to intercede for mankind before the heavenly Father. As a member of the Godhead, He knew what heaven was all about and how to tell us what to expect and how to live in a way that was acceptable to the Father, making the right choices that would bring forth a spiritual life and produce the love of God in us.

I like the way Jesus expressed the unity and joint purpose of Himself and the Father in the following scripture. "I and My Father are one" (John 10:30, NKJ). The scriptures we have just discussed give us a glimpse of who Jesus was and that He was sent by the Father. Let's review the necessity of His coming to earth. It will help us keep things in perspective. At any rate, it will help me keep things in perspective.

Jesus came to earth to redeem mankind from his sins. When we read in the Old Testament about all those blood sacrifices, it can be pretty gory. There seems to be blood everywhere. The reason blood is so important is because "life" is in the blood. In the following scripture, God is giving Noah instructions not to eat the flesh of animals without draining the blood first. "But you shall not eat flesh with its life, that is, its blood" (Genesis 9:4, NKJ). In a spiritual sense, blood has a voice and can cry out. In this next scripture, God is speaking to Cain, one of Adam's sons, after Cain killed his brother. "And He said, 'What have you done? The voice of your brother's blood cries out to Me from the ground. So now you are cursed from the earth, which has opened its mouth to receive your brother's blood from your hand'" (Genesis 4:10-11). The blood of Jesus was perfect and pure. Jesus was the ultimate sacrifice. There could be no other.

> Not with the blood of goats and calves, but with His own blood He entered the Most Holy Place once for all, having obtained eternal redemption. For if the blood of bulls and goats and the ashes of a heifer, sprinkling the unclean, sanctifies for the purifying of the flesh, how much more shall the blood of Christ, who through the eternal Spirit offered Himself without spot

to God, cleanse your conscience from dead works to serve the living God?

—Hebrews 9:12-14 (nkj)

We tend to treat sin as an "oops" in our life. Our hearts have hardened to the holiness of God. Many of us have heard the resurrection story from childhood, and it is easy to develop a casual attitude in breaking our heavenly Father's commands. It is always good for us to reflect on the price that was paid for our eternal soul. It was the Father's pleasure to have sent Jesus to us, and He is always ready to forgive us. The key is to not keep sinning and wearing out God's grace. "If we confess our sins, He is faithful and just to forgive us our sins and to cleanse us from all unrighteousness" (1 John 1:9, nkj).

Now we are ready to get down to the business of Jesus and His mission of love in coming to the earth. "Now after John was put into prison, Jesus came to Galilee, preaching the gospel of the kingdom of God, and saying, 'The time is fulfilled, and the kingdom of God is at hand. Repent, and believe in the gospel'" (Mark 1:14-15, nkj). Jesus not only came to save us from our sins and be a sacrifice, but while He was here, He told us about His Father and His kingdom (heaven). Jesus also told us how to live and act as citizens of this heavenly kingdom while we are here on earth.

After all, we are the light of God that shines in a dark world, pointing the way to Christ. What is the main ingredient of this kingdom? It is *love*. Jesus is talking to some of the religious leaders in the following scripture.

> Then one of the scribes came, and having heard them reasoning together, perceiving that He had answered them well, asked Him, "Which is the first commandment of all?" Jesus answered him, "The first of all the commandments is: 'Hear, O Israel, the Lord our God, the Lord is one. And you shall love the Lord your God with all your heart, with all your soul, with all your mind, and with all your strength.' This is the first commandment. And the second, like it, is this: 'You shall love your neighbor as yourself.' There is no other commandment greater than these." So the scribe said to Him, "Well said, Teacher. You have spoken the truth, for there is one God, and there is no other but He. And to love Him with all the heart, with all the understanding, with all the soul, and with all the strength, and to love one's neighbor as oneself, is more than all the whole burnt offerings and sacrifices." Now when Jesus saw that he answered wisely, he said to him, "You are

not far from the kingdom of God." But after that no one dared question Him.

—Mark 12:28-34 (NKJ)

This is the gospel and the kingdom of God summed up in just a few words, but isn't it interesting how it all boils down to love! Remember, God is Love; therefore, His kingdom and His gospel is also love. Obeying these commandments of love fulfills the Ten Commandments that were given to Moses in the Old Testament. Jesus is speaking in the following scripture. "On these two commandments hang all the Law and the Prophets" (Matthew 22:40, NKJ). In loving the heavenly Father and then loving others, love can come full circle because our source of love is in God. By keeping our "love connection" with the source of love (God), hate will have no room to grow. Jesus said He did not come to destroy the Law but to fulfill the Law. "Do not think that I came to destroy the Law or the Prophets. I did not come to destroy but to fulfill. For assuredly, I say to you, till heaven and earth pass away, one jot or one tittle will by no means pass from the law till all is fulfilled" (Matthew 5:17-18). Love fulfills that law, and Jesus shows us the way.

One of the most important and greatest sermons preached by Jesus was known as the "Sermon on the Mount." Jesus brought a new kind of teaching. He was preparing us for the age of grace. Instead of an "eye for an eye," forgiveness was to be given.

God is not so much impressed with the outward appearance or works of man, as what is in man's heart. The message of the Sermon on the Mount begins in Matthew 5 and goes through Matthew 7. Since this book is about the Father's love, I have chosen a few of the scriptures that deal directly with love and our conduct toward others and God. The first scripture is on loving your enemies. Jesus is speaking in the following scripture.

> You have heard that it was said, "You shall love your neighbor and hate your enemy." But I say to you, love your enemies, bless those who curse you, do good to those who hate you, and pray for those who spitefully use you and persecute you, that you may be sons of your Father in heaven; for He makes His sun rise on the evil and on the good, and sends rain on the just and on the unjust. For if you love those who love you, what reward have you? Do not even the tax collectors do the same? And if you greet your brethren only, what do you do more than others? Do not even the tax collectors do so? Therefore you shall be perfect, just as your Father in heaven is perfect.
>
> —Matthew 5:43-48 (NKJ)

It is easy to love those who love us. It is a lot more challenging to reach out to a stranger or be nice to a nasty person who is deliberately trying to do you harm. Just think of that social-climbing coworker who spends his or her time trying to get you into trouble on the job. Maybe the coworker is full of pain and has no one to show him or her the love of God. If you don't, who will?

Perhaps there is a grouchy, grumpy person (young or old) lurking in the neighborhood that couldn't put a smile on their face even if God came down and tickled him or her with a feather. If you see that person coming, is it time to look down and keep walking? What if that person just needs a friend and is very lonely and hurting? If you don't show them the love of God, who will? What would a smile cost at this point? You may have just been the best thing that happened to that person all day.

How about that drunk on the corner with a bottle in his hand, making the neighborhood look bad and causing the property value to go down? It is way too easy to cross the street to avoid this unpleasant, smelly person. After all, they may ask for money.

Believe it or not, Jesus loves these people, and the love of God commands that we love these people, too. Remember that even one of the disciples of Jesus was a tax collector, which was one of the most despised professions of that day. One of

His disciples was even a thief. This is where love excels. Are we not God's hands extended? Here we are in these scriptures, being given a charge by Jesus, the Son of God, to go and love our enemies. This is a painful task and not an easy one, but it will please the Father.

The choice is ours. This is a part of what love is. Jesus is speaking in this scripture. "For if you forgive men their trespasses, your heavenly Father will also forgive you. But if you do not forgive men their trespasses, neither will your Father forgive your trespasses" (Matthew 6:14-15, NKJ). Loving our enemies and forgiving those who have wronged us are probably two of the most difficult things for us to do in our flesh. It is painful and takes a lot of effort in the beginning.

Jesus came into a world that hated Him, so that He could forgive them. Jesus forgave the people who put Him on the cross. Couldn't we at least make an effort, if not for ourselves then for the sake of the kingdom of God, to forgive others when we have been wronged and see people through the eyes of Jesus? In order for us to love on a level like this, we need to understand what love is about and what Jesus had in mind in His teaching about the kingdom of God. We need to receive this love in our hearts. This book is about understanding— to understand more about love so that we, in our own lives, can mirror the love of the Father through Jesus Christ, who is our example.

Jesus also gave us some direction on giving or doing charitable deeds.

> Take heed that you do not do your charitable deeds before men, to be seen by them. Otherwise you have no reward from your Father in heaven. Therefore, when you do a charitable deed, do not sound a trumpet before you as the hypocrites do in the synagogues and in the streets, that they may have glory from men. Assuredly, I say to you, they have their reward. But when you do a charitable deed, do not let your left hand know what your right hand is doing, that your charitable deed may be in secret; and your Father who sees in secret will Himself reward you openly.
>
> —Matthew 6:1-4 (NKJ)

Man looks on the outward appearance, but God looks on the heart. We have a saying in our society that says, "Seeing is believing." For a Christian, that is not a true statement, for we walk by faith and not by sight. If we do a good deed just to be noticed by men, our reward for that good deed will be made void in heaven. Part of this is pride in action. We want people to see how much we give for an offering or do in good works just to get attention so that people will think that we are righteous. Our flesh is in action, and our purpose will fail.

> Now Jesus sat opposite the treasury and saw how the people put money into the treasury. And many who were rich put in much. Then one poor widow came and threw in two mites, which make a quadrans. So He called His disciples to Himself and said to them, "Assuredly, I say to you that this poor widow has put in more than all those who have given to the treasury; for they all put in out of their abundance, but she out of her poverty put in all that she had, her whole livelihood."

> —Mark 12:41-44 (NKJ)

God cares about the motive of the heart. We give because we want to honor God. The amount is between the Lord and the individual. We do charitable work and volunteer work because we want to share the love of God with others. This is true motivation. Man cannot see into the heart, but God does. Don't be entrapped by social behavior or standards that God has not given. His love is real, not just a social protocol.

In preaching the kingdom of God, Jesus didn't address the cares and possessions of this world nearly as much as our behavior in readiness and alignment for life in heaven. Remember, this world was made by God for man to have dominion over the earth with the intent of the heavenly Father having His creation with Him as a family. In the beginning, the earth was created in perfection. The life we live down here is like a vapor or a blade of grass—"here today and gone tomorrow." Never forget God's original intent for mankind. Don't lose this vision that our Father has for us. This vision will not change but will be fulfilled in its original intent. In understanding your heavenly Father's love, this point is essential. Again I say never forget the original vision or intent of the heavenly Father for you, which is to be with Him for eternity. To begin to understand this point with your heart is to begin to understand the Father's love for you to where you can put your relationship with Him into better perspective.

The choices we make down here on earth in our life, the way we love God and others, all determine our eternal life. The possessions that we have down here and all our material goods will pass away. I am sure you have heard the expression, "You can't take it with you." How true it is. Only what is done for Christ will last. Jesus is speaking in the following scripture.

> Do not lay up for yourselves treasures on earth, where moth and rust destroy and where thieves break in and steal; but lay up for yourselves treasures in heaven, where

neither moth nor rust destroys and where thieves do not break in and steal. For where your treasure is, there your heart will be also.

—Matthew 6:19-21 (NKJ)

This thought goes right along with what Jesus said when He told us not to worry. The economic times back then were a lot worse than now. Israel was under Roman law and authority. Poverty was everywhere. Jesus was preaching to the poor of that day even more so than the rich. This message is just as true for us today.

Therefore I say to you, do not worry about your life, what you will eat or what you will drink; nor about your body, what you will put on. Is not life more than food and the body more than clothing? Look at the birds of the air, for they neither sow nor reap nor gather into barns; yet your heavenly Father feeds them. Are you not of more value than they? Which of you by worrying can add one cubit to his stature? So why do you worry about clothing? Consider the lilies of the field, how they grow: they neither toil nor spin; and yet I say to you that even Solomon in all his glory was not arrayed like one of these. Now if God so clothes the grass of the field, which today is, and tomorrow is thrown into the oven, will He not much more clothe you, O you of little faith? Therefore do not worry, saying, 'What shall we eat,' or 'What shall we drink,' or 'What shall we wear?' For after all these things the Gentiles seek. For your heavenly Father knows that you need all these things. But seek first the kingdom of God and His righteousness, and all these things shall be added to you. Therefore do not worry about tomorrow, for tomorrow will worry about its own things. Sufficient for the day is its own trouble.

—Matthew 6:25-34 (NKJ)

This is a great promise of love from our heavenly Father. God still wants to take care of us. He does not want us to worry about material things. He gives us all things. However, it is hard for us because we do put our trust in our possessions.

Our Lord's goal for us here on earth is not to make us all millionaires. We are to be like Jesus, love the Father, love others, and carry out the business of the kingdom of God. Our life on earth is temporary. The condition of the Lord meeting our needs is that we seek first the kingdom of God.

Worry is a form of fear. It will make you sick. Worry is also unbelief. I know this is hard. I have trouble trusting the Lord at times for my provision.

Because we lack faith does not mean that the promise God made to us is not real. It is important to God and Jesus that you believe what has been said in the scriptures. The Lord knows the times are hard, and He doesn't want His children to fret but wants you to believe Him when He says He will take care of you. Determine in your heart to trust Him for your needs. There are no magic tricks involved and no secret keys to follow. Just love your Lord and seek His kingdom. It is that simple, and yet it is that hard. God wants our hearts and our energies focused on the things of God. In the following scripture, Jesus is speaking to a crowd the day after He had fed 5,000 people by a miracle. The crowd had followed Him for the wrong reasons. They were fed a free meal.

> Jesus answered them and said, "Most assuredly, I say to you, you seek Me, not because you saw the signs, but because you ate of the loaves and were filled. Do not labor for the food which perishes, but for the food which endures to everlasting life, which the Son of Man will give you, because God the Father has set His seal on Him."

> —John 6:26-27 (NKJ)

In revealing Himself to us as the Messiah and ushering in a new covenant, Jesus broke a lot of social barriers of His day. One of the forbidden groups of people to be around was the Samaritans. Jesus had an encounter with a woman from Samaria, demonstrating that the kingdom of God would be extended to other peoples and nations.

> Now Jacob's well was there. Jesus therefore, being wearied from His journey, sat thus by the well. It was about the sixth hour. A woman of Samaria came to draw water. Jesus said to her, "Give Me a drink." For His disciples had gone away into the city to buy food. Then the woman of Samaria said to Him, "How is it that You, being a Jew, ask a drink from me, a Samaritan woman?" For Jews have no dealings with Samaritans. Jesus answered and said to her, "If you knew the gift of God, and who it is who says to you, 'Give Me a drink,' you would have asked Him, and He would have given you living water." The woman said to Him, "Sir, You have nothing to draw with, and the well is deep. Where then do You get that living water? Are You greater than our father Jacob, who gave us the well, and drank from it himself, as well as his sons and his livestock?" Jesus answered and said to her, "Whoever drinks of this water will thirst again, but whoever drinks of the water that I shall give him will never thirst. But the water that I shall give him will

become in him a fountain of water springing up into everlasting life." The woman said to Him, "Sir, give me this water that I may not thirst, nor come here to draw." Jesus said to her, "Go, call your husband, and come here." The woman answered and said, "I have no husband." Jesus said to her, "You have well said, 'I have no husband,' for you have had five husbands, and the one whom you now have is not your husband; in that you spoke truly." The woman said to Him, "Sir, I perceive that You are a prophet. Our fathers worshiped on this the mountain, and you Jews say that in Jerusalem is the place where one ought to worship." Jesus said to her, "Woman, believe Me, the hour is coming when you will neither on this mountain, nor in Jerusalem, worship the Father. You worship what you do not know; we know what we worship, for salvation is of the Jews. But the hour is coming, and now is, when the true worshipers will worship the Father in spirit and truth; for the Father is seeking such to worship Him. God is Spirit, and those who worship Him must worship in spirit and truth." The woman said to Him, "I know that Messiah is coming (who is called Christ). When He comes, He will tell us all things." Jesus said to her, "I who speak to you am He." And at this point His disciples came, and they marveled that He talked with a woman; yet not one said, "What do You seek?" or, "Why are You talking with her?" The woman then left her water pot, went her way into the city, and said to the men, "Come, see a Man who told me all things that I ever did. Could this be the Christ?"

—John 4:6-29 (NKJ)

This group of people later accepted Jesus as the Messiah. "Then they said to the woman, 'Now we believe, not because of what you said, for we ourselves have heard Him and we know that this is indeed the Christ, the Savior of the world'" (John 4:42, NKJ). I love this account of love! I can almost feel the hunger of the woman of Samaria to know the truth, and I loved how childlike she was in believing the words that Jesus spoke. This group of people readily believed that Jesus was the Messiah.

Jesus was preparing the disciples and Jews to get ready for some changes under this "new covenant" that He was bringing into the world. The gospel would also be offered to the Gentiles; it was not just for Jews, only. This must have been a very challenging concept for the disciples to comprehend at that time. Nothing like this had been taught before. Jesus explains to the woman that worshipers will not just worship God in the place where she is or in Jerusalem, but true worship will take place anywhere and everywhere. People will worship God in spirit and in truth. Therefore, all the earth will be filled with the glory of the Lord.

Another event that is recorded about Jesus crossing the social barriers is found in the story of the woman from Canaan.

> Then Jesus went out from there and departed to the region of Tyre and Sidon. And behold , a woman of Canaan came from that region and cried out to Him, saying, "Have mercy on me, O Lord, son of David! My daughter is severely demon-possessed." But He answered her not a word. And His disciples came and urged Him, saying, "Send her away, for she cries out after us." But He answered and said, "I was not sent except to the lost sheep of the house of Israel." Then she came and worshipped Him, saying, "Lord help me!" But He answered and said, "It is not good to take the children's bread and throw it to the little dogs." And she said, "Yes, Lord, yet even the little dogs eat the crumbs which fall from their masters' table." Then Jesus answered and said to her. "O woman, great is your faith! Let it be to you as you desire." And her daughter was healed from that very hour.

> —Matthew 15:21-28 (NKJ)

One would think that Jesus was being hard on this woman who was filled with so much pain and desperation. I believe that Jesus was testing her faith and love. God has a right to do that with each of His children, and sometimes He does. This account is a beautiful and emotional story of love. She passed the test that Jesus gave her. I can almost see the smile on Jesus's face when she answered Him. Her faith did not waiver. She did not get insulted and walk away. Love does not give up. She knew that Jesus was the answer. Even though she was not a Jew, she had hope in the God of the Jews. She was not turned away. This is love in action.

In the following scripture, Jesus stresses the point of hearing His word and doing what he teaches (practice His sayings). The following people actually performed miracles in His name, but they did not practice His teachings in their own lives, and therefore the miracles were to no avail.

> Not everyone who says to Me, "Lord, Lord," shall enter the kingdom of heaven, but he who does the will of My Father in heaven. Many will say to Me in that day, "Lord, Lord, have we not prophesied in Your name, cast out demons in Your name, and done many wonders in Your name?" And then I will declare to them, "I never knew you; depart from Me, you who practice lawlessness!" Therefore whoever

hears these sayings of Mine, and does them, I will liken him to a wise man who built his house on the rock: and the rain descended, the floods came, and the winds blew and beat on that house; and it did not fall, for it was founded on the rock. But everyone who hears these sayings of Mine, and does not do them, will be like a foolish man who built his house on the sand: and the rain descended, the floods came, and the winds blew and beat on that house; and it fell. And great was its fall.

—Matthew 7:21-27 (NKJ)

Jesus came with words of life for man. He is the door, and no man can get to heaven, except through the Son. He is the way, the truth, and the life. There is no other way. In the previous scripture, Jesus is talking to those who practiced an outward religion. They looked good on the outside and seemed very religious, but they did not practice the teachings of Jesus. They were like the foolish man who built his house on the sand. God knows their heart and the fruit they bear. He knows our heart and the fruit we bear. Just a good outward appearance can't fool God, who sees into the soul.

In this chapter we have discovered that Jesus was qualified as the Son of God. He was God but became a man to become our High Priest and make Himself a perfect sacrifice for all of mankind. Only

His blood could atone and wipe out the sins of man. Only Jesus was qualified for this task, and He did it of His own free will. We discussed how Jesus and the Father are one. Jesus is a part of the Godhead and has always been in existence with the Father, yet Jesus said He could do nothing without the Father. They are in complete agreement.

We looked at the two greatest commandments that Jesus gave: to love God and to love others as ourselves. Jesus said that on these two commandments hang all the law and prophets. Love is the key ingredient. Jesus preached the kingdom of God. He taught us how to love and to conduct ourselves toward God and then others. The Sermon on the Mount is all about teaching us how to live an acceptable life before God. The Lord did not want us to fret about our lives down here. He commanded us not to worry because the heavenly Father would take care of our needs. The condition is that we would obey and serve Him by seeking first the kingdom of heaven. Our lives down here on earth are nothing compared to what awaits us in heaven. Jesus showed us that the kingdom of God would be extended to the Gentiles as well as the Jews. He broke social barriers with his discussion with the woman of Samaria and the woman from Canaan. The message of the Messiah was breaking cultural boundaries that seemed unimaginable in that day.

Love was and always will be the key that breaks the barriers between man and God and man and man. Jesus continued the message of His Father in teaching us that we need to make the right choices and live a holy and righteous life before Him. God will not tolerate disobedience, but the obedient will have eternal life.

His words and parables were all about the choices we make. He truly preached the kingdom of God. Jesus said if we obey his sayings, we are like a wise man who built his house on the rock, and when the winds and rain came, the house did not fall. Jesus points us to the Father and to His love. Jesus is our sacrificial lamb, teacher, rabbi, high priest, brother, father, sister, mother, beginning, end, lover, and lover of our soul. He is worthy of our praise.

WHAT IS LOVE?

*T*here is one chapter in the Bible that is dedicated to telling us the meaning of love. It is I Corinthians 13. It not only defines some of the characteristics of our heavenly Father and Jesus but also is a standard and a guide for us on how to love God and others.

> If I [can] speak in the tongues of men and
> [even] of angels, but have not love (that
> reasoning, intentional, spiritual devotion
> such as is inspired by God's love for and
> in us), I am only a noisy gong or a clanging
> cymbal. And if I have prophetic powers—
> that is, the gift of interpreting the divine
> will and purpose; and understand all the
> secret truths and mysteries and possess all
> knowledge, and if I have (sufficient) faith
> so that I can remove mountains, but have
> not love [God's love in me] I am nothing—a

useless nobody. Even if I dole out all that I have [to the poor in providing] food, and if I surrender my body to be burned [or in order that I may glory], but have not love (God's love in me), I gain nothing. Love endures long and is patient and kind; love never is envious nor boils over with jealousy; is not boastful or vainglorious, does not display itself haughtily. It is not conceited—arrogant and inflated with pride; it is not rude (unmannerly), and does not act unbecomingly. Love (God's love in us) does not insist on its own rights or its own way, for it is not self-seeking; it is not touchy or fretful or resentful; it takes no account of the evil done to it—pays no attention to a suffered wrong. It does not rejoice at injustice and unrighteousness, but rejoices when right and truth prevail. Love bears up under anything and everything that comes, is ever ready to believe the best of every person, its hopes are fadeless under all circumstances and it endures everything [without weakening]. Love never fails—never fades out or becomes obsolete or comes to an end. As for prophecy [that is, the gift of interpreting the divine will and purpose], it will be fulfilled and pass away; as for tongues, they will be destroyed and cease; as for knowledge, it will pass away [it will lose its value and be superseded by truth]. For our knowledge is fragmentary (incomplete and imperfect), and our prophecy (our teaching) is fragmentary (incomplete and imperfect). But when the complete and perfect [total] comes, the incomplete and imperfect will vanish away—become antiquated, void and superseded. When I was a child, I talked like a child, I thought like a child, I reasoned like a child; now that I have become a man, I am done with childish ways and have put them aside. For now we are looking in a mirror that gives only a dim (blurred) reflection [of reality as in a riddle or enigma], but then [when perfection comes] we shall see in reality and face to face! Now I know in part (imperfectly); but then I shall know and understand fully and clearly, even in the same manner as I have been fully and clearly known and understood [by God]. And so faith, hope, love abide; [faith, conviction and belief respecting man's relation to God and divine things; hope, joyful and confident expectation of eternal salvation; love, true affection for God and man, growing out of God's love for and in us], these three, but the greatest of these is love.

—1 Corinthians 13:1-13 (Amplified)

Remember, to love is not a suggestion. It is a commandment. The apostle Paul writes that without God's love in us, we are nothing. No matter what accomplishments we can do on this earth and how much we try to do in humanitarian works, without the love of God in us, it all is futile. It doesn't matter how smart we are, how good looking we are, or even how thin we are. Even the working of miracles is of no effect without love. We will not be able to fool God with an outward appearance of good works or even just by going to church every Sunday. God sees the heart. He knows what is on the inside.

Jesus is speaking in the following scripture about the end of days. "Many will say to Me in that day, 'Lord, Lord, have we not prophesied in Your name, cast out demons in Your name, and done many wonders in Your name?' And then I will declare to them, 'I never knew you; depart from Me, you who practice lawlessness!'" (Matthew 7:22-23, NKJ)

To do miracles or even be used in the gifts of the Spirit is fruitless unless love is in our hearts. God wants a love relationship with mankind, and He wants us to give Him and other people the same kind of love that He has given to us.

Can you envision a loving father who does all for his children, and they just go about their lives taking from the father's hand, not returning any of the generosity that has been given to them? There is no love, compassion, or kindness shown in return. They show up for meals and family outings as requested, but they are distant and uncaring. This does not sound very appealing, even in the natural, and yet this is the way we, at times, treat God.

There is no substitute for love and affection. Your heavenly Father never gets tired of hearing you say that you love Him.

"Love endures long and is patient and kind" (1 Corinthians 13:4a, Amplified). Love doesn't always come easily. Emotional pain can be involved. Our emotions and our flesh get in the way. We have to understand the bigger picture of love, put our flesh down, and choose to do the right thing.

Think of how patient our Lord was with the disciples. They were raw material to work with. Yet for three years, Jesus taught them the principles of the kingdom of God so that they could pass it on to us. The disciples made plenty of mistakes, but Jesus was persistent to keep them on track. Think of Jesus, a perfect man who knew the secrets of the kingdom of heaven, taking up the task to teach twelve unlearned men the principles of love. At times in the scriptures we can see Jesus a little frustrated with the disciples for moving in fleshly ways, but He never stopped loving them, and He never gave up on them. He entrusted them with a great burden when He ascended into heaven. That trust was not misplaced because we have all seen the outcome.

Love "never is envious, or boils over with jealousy" (1 Corinthians 13:4a, Amplified). It is mentioned several times in the gospels that the disciples would argue among themselves about who was the greatest. One situation that comes to mind was when the mother of the sons of Zebedee came to Jesus and asked that, when Jesus came into His kingdom, for one son to sit at His right and the other son to sit at his left hand. Jesus explained to her that it was the Father who made that decision. The other ten disciples were upset with the brothers for trying to assert themselves into such a position. Jesus called them together for a team meeting. The following scripture demonstrates the attitude of our Lord, and we would be wise to follow in His steps.

> But Jesus called them to Himself and said, "You know that the rulers of the Gentiles lord it over them, and those who are great exercise authority over them. Yet it shall not be so among you; but whoever desires to become great among you, let him be your servant. And whoever desires to be first among you, let him be your slave—just as the Son of Man did not come to be served, but to serve, and to give His life a ransom for many."
>
> —Matthew 20:25-28 (NKJ)

Love "is not boastful or vainglorious, does not display itself haughtily" (1 Corinthians 13:4b, Amplified). The birth of Jesus was far from a regal display. He was born to poor parents. He was put in a manger for a bed. Shepherds were alerted by the singing of angels; otherwise, it was a quiet night. Most of the people had no idea of what was happening. Jesus, as He was growing up, learned the trade of a carpenter. Our Lord lived a life of humility and never asserted His real position to influence or sway people. Jesus told a parable that summed up this thought nicely.

> Also He spoke this parable to some who trusted in themselves that they were righteous, and despised others: "Two men went up to the temple to pray, one a Pharisee and the other a tax collector. The Pharisee stood and prayed thus with himself, 'God, I thank You that I am not like other men—extortioners, unjust, adulterers, or even as this tax collector. I fast twice a week; I give tithes of all that I possess.' And the tax collector, standing afar off, would not so much as raise his eyes to heaven, but beat his breast, saying, 'God, be merciful to me a sinner!' I tell you, this man went down to his house justified rather than the other; for everyone who exalts himself will

be humbled, and he who humbles himself will be exalted."

—Luke 18:9-14 (NKJ)

God loves all people, even in their sin, and He loves us even in our sin. God loves the person next to you as much as He loves you and as much as He loves Jesus. This is who God is—love. God loves the worst sinner as much as He loves the most obedient saint. Our earthly position doesn't mean anything to God since He is the one who gives us all things. We cannot judge people by the outward appearance. Only the Father knows their heart and what has brought them to where they are. Let the compassion of Jesus guide you.

Love, "it is not conceited—arrogant and inflated with pride" (1 Corinthians 13:5a, Amplified). After being baptized by John the Baptist, Jesus was led by the Holy Spirit into the wilderness to be tempted by the devil. Jesus had fasted for forty days and nights, and then the devil came to Him and tempted Him three times. Here is the Son of God, submitting Himself as a man to be tested by the enemy of God. Jesus did not have to remind the devil of who He was. One word from Jesus, and the devil would be put down. Our Lord knew what was at stake. Jesus had nothing to lose, but we did; therefore, Jesus held His peace and, in perfect wisdom, answered the devil with scripture the three times He was confronted.

Now when the tempter came to Him, he said, "If You are the Son of God, command that these stones become bread." But He answered and said, "It is written, 'Man shall not live by bread alone, but by every word that proceeds from the mouth of God.'" Then the devil took Him up into the holy city, set Him on the pinnacle of the temple, and said to Him, "If You are the Son of God, throw Yourself down. For it is written: 'He shall give His angels charge over you,' and 'In their hands they shall bear you up, lest you dash your foot against a stone.'" Jesus said to him, "It is written again, 'You shall not tempt the Lord your God.'" Again, the devil took Him up on an exceedingly high mountain, and showed Him all the kingdoms of the world and their glory. And he said to Him, "All these things I will give You if You will fall down and worship me." Then Jesus said to him, "Away with you, Satan! For it is written, 'You shall worship the Lord your God, and Him only you shall serve.'" Then the devil left Him, and behold, angels came and ministered to Him.

—Matthew 4:3-11 (NKJ)

In each of the three times that the devil came to Jesus, not once did Jesus assert His position as the

Son of God. He was facing the devil as a man—and for mankind. The devil wanted Jesus to focus on the fact that He was the Son of God—more than a man. Our Lord could have called for angels to come at any time. Jesus remembered His place and the plan of the Father. That's love!

Some people who have aggressive behavior or people who are in places of authority or power in this world are known to blurt out statements like, "Do you know who you are talking to?" and "Who do you think you are, talking to me like that? I know more than you'll ever know about that subject!" We spend our lives trying to find a place on this planet where we can feel safe. When our position or safe place is threatened, we can all come out fighting like tigers. Welcome to the human race. However, Jesus had a better idea in not pushing His position or having to lift Himself up to make a point. He knew when to keep silent, and when He spoke it was the heavenly Father speaking through Him. We would be wise to do the same.

Love, "it is not rude (unmannerly), and does not act unbecomingly" (1 Corinthians 13:5a, Amplified). As a Jew, Jesus did a few things that were "un-kosher" for His time. He crossed the barriers of race and gender to reach all of the people. Jesus treated everyone the same—with love. He talked to a woman of Samaria, a Roman centurion, lepers, and a prostitute just to mention a few. The

Jews were not to have anything to do with these types of people. Even though His first mission was to the Jewish people, He saw the big picture that eventually all could come and gain entrance to the kingdom of God. This behavior appalled the religious Jews as well as the commoners.

Jesus introduced us to a "new covenant" that was not necessarily destroying the law but fulfilling it. Our Lord was tearing down walls and building bridges of love that would reach to all mankind. This is what the Father had wanted from the beginning, and Jesus was showing us the way. "And I say to you that many will come from east and west and sit down with Abraham, Isaac, and Jacob in the kingdom of heaven" (Matthew 8:11, NKJ).

Did you know that you are an ambassador of Jesus Christ and the kingdom of God? When people see you, they should see Jesus. The Spirit of the Lord is in you. Jesus came into your heart to live when you accepted Him as Lord and Savior. Therefore, our actions and reactions should reflect that of the kingdom of God. How have you done as His ambassador today?

"Love [God's love in us] does not insist on its own rights or its own way, for it is not self-seeking; it is not touchy or fretful or resentful" (1 Corinthians 13:5b, Amplified). It is amazing that Jesus, being part man and part God, was as humble as He was. He was a rightful heir of heaven, yet our Lord chose, of His own free will, to submit Himself to the father. Jesus is speaking in the following scripture. "I can of myself do nothing. As I hear, I judge; and My judgment is righteous, because I do not seek My own will but the will of the Father who sent Me" (John 5:30, NKJ). Didn't Jesus just say that He could do nothing without the Father? To me this shows the love and devotion between the Father and the Son. They are separate, and yet they operate as one in total agreement. It gives a new meaning to the phrase "perfect harmony."

Jesus is speaking in the following scripture. "For I have come down from heaven, not to do My own will, but the will of Him who sent Me" (John 6:38, NKJ). There is only one will that prevails, and that is the will of the Father. Jesus knew how to reverence His heavenly Father, and we should do likewise.

I was very headstrong and stubborn when I was younger. "Do it my way!" Needless to say, I had to change my heart and my attitude. It just seemed like things went so much better when I had full control...or so I thought. Actually, nothing went better. As a matter of fact, things always got worse. No one wins when people control and manipulate every situation they can.

Love, "it takes no account of the evil done to it—pays no attention to a suffered wrong" (1 Corinthians 13:5c, Amplified). This is a difficult scripture to try to live out. When we are wronged, the first instinct is to lash out. We feel that we have been betrayed. Our memories can sometimes be

THE GREATEST OF THESE IS LOVE

our worst enemy. This is where forgiveness comes in. When people do us wrong or come against us, it is important to forgive. I am not saying this lightly, and I do not mean to be harsh. As we explore more about the kingdom of God, hopefully this will become clearer as to why the Father has asked this of us. Many people are filled with pain caused by thoughtless or evil people. The Lord has made it very clear that to be forgiven we must forgive.

Jesus is speaking in the following scripture. "For if you forgive men their trespasses, your heavenly Father will also forgive you. But if you do not forgive men their trespasses, neither will your Father forgive your trespasses" (Matthew 6:14-15, NKJ). The greatest example of forgiveness is Jesus on the cross. "Then Jesus said, 'Father, forgive them, for they do not know what they do'" (Luke 23:34a, NKJ). Think of all the pain He was suffering, not to mention the ridicule and hate that was put upon Him. He had not done any wrong. Yet of His own free will, He chose to forgive his enemies even as He was dying. This is His greatest testimony of love known to mankind. Jesus came as a human sacrifice to save the very people who hung Him on the cross. The blood of Jesus covers mankind from Adam's generation to the generations to come. Even today there are people who would hang Jesus on the cross again. But Jesus chose to go to the cross so that those who would call out to Him—just as the thief on the cross did—would be with Him in heaven.

Love, "it does not rejoice at injustice and unrighteousness, but rejoices when right and truth prevail" (1 Corinthians 13:6, Amplified). A good example of this sign of love would be Jesus and the adulteress.

> Then the scribes and Pharisees brought to Him a woman caught in adultery. And when they had set her in the midst, they said to Him, "Teacher, this woman was caught in adultery, in the very act. Now Moses, in the law, commanded us that such should be stoned. But what do you say?" This they said, testing Him, that they might have something of which to accuse Him. But Jesus stooped down and wrote on the ground with His finger, as though He did not hear. So when they continued asking Him, He raised Himself up and said to them, "He who is without sin, among you, let him throw a stone at her first." And again He stooped down and wrote on the ground. Then those who heard it, being convicted by their conscience, went out one by one, beginning with the oldest even to the last. And Jesus was left alone, and the woman standing in the midst. When Jesus had raised Himself up and saw no one but the woman, He said to her, "Woman, where are those accusers of yours? Has no one condemned you?" She said, "No one

Lord" And Jesus said to her, "Neither do I condemn you; go and sin no more."

—John 8:3-11 (NKJ)

The men who brought the woman to Jesus were vindictive. They were looking for a reason to accuse Jesus—even at the expense of this woman's life. They had as much sin in their own lives. There was more to what was happening here than a woman caught in adultery. Jesus knew what they were up to. By asking them to examine their own sin before judging the woman, He brought the truth to light, and it did prevail. After looking at their own lives, they could not throw a stone at the woman to condemn her. Jesus did not condone what the woman did. However, he told her that He did not condemn her and then told her to go and sin no more. She also had some soul searching to do.

This really displays the wisdom of our Lord and His love. Sometimes we as Christians can be a little judgmental. Instead of using the Bible as a guide for our life, we tend to use it as a hammer to hit our neighbor over the head if we see a wrong in their life. We forget to mix grace and wisdom in our observations. Only God can see the heart. The Holy Spirit is our guide, and our job is not to judge our neighbor. "Judge not, and you shall not be judged. Condemn not, and you shall not be condemned. Forgive, and you will be forgiven" (Luke 6:37, NKJ).

"Love bears up under anything and everything that comes, is ever ready to believe the best of every person, its hopes are fadeless under all circumstances and it endures everything [without weakening]" (1 Corinthians 13:7, Amplified). What better example is there of this kind of love than Jesus on the cross? He bore the sins of each and every person who was born since Adam to the last person that will be born on the earth. He endured beatings, ridicule, and abuse that we can't even begin to imagine. His disciples and friends left Him alone. He was betrayed by Judas, who was with Him in ministry. As we have just read, Love is ready to believe the best of every person. Jesus was leaving, in the hands of His disciples, the future of the church and the finishing of the work that He had begun.

Think of the huge responsibility that these eleven disciples had. Can you imagine what would have happened if the disciples lost interest or decided the task was too much for them? I would think that Jesus would be a little nervous to give mankind a second chance of not making the same mistakes in disobedience that Adam did. To begin with, at the time of Genesis, Adam messed up by eating the fruit of the tree of knowledge of good and evil. The heavenly Father, Jesus, and the Holy Spirit had faith that mankind would be able to continue the gospel message that Jesus started and to spread the redemption message throughout the whole world. How about in this present day? Does the love in our hearts bear all things and believe all things? Do we believe the best in every person? Every person has to judge himself in this area. I am willing to guess that we all could use some growth in love. The good news is that the growth in love is in us, and all we have to do is ask for it.

This world is imperfect. Our bodies and our minds are imperfect. The knowledge and understanding we have is limited and imperfect, as well. When our Lord returns to earth, all things will be restored and made complete. "But when the complete and perfect [total] comes, the incomplete and imperfect will vanish away—become antiquated, void and superseded" (1 Corinthians 13:10, Amplified). When the Lord returns, we shall know reality and have full understanding because all of the walls and obstacles will be removed between the Godhead and us.

> And so faith, hope, love abide; [faith, conviction and belief respecting man's relation to God and divine things; hope, joyful and confident expectation of eternal salvation; love, true affection for God and man, growing out of God's love for and in us], these three, but the greatest of these is love.
>
> —1 Corinthians 13:13 (Amplified)

How true this is. Of all things, material possessions, political ambitions, wealth—whatever we can conceive to be great and important—it will all turn to rubble in the end. Love, real love, God's love is all that really matters. It is all that will last.

First Corinthians 13 describes the character of God in the fact that God is love. This is the kind of love that He shows to us and wants us to show to others. We have identified some of the definitions of love, what love consists of, and in some cases, the sacrifices that we need to make for love. Without love we are nothing. Our lives would be without meaning. Even though we may be intelligent, have great wealth, or even are used greatly in ministry, if we do not have love, it is to no avail. If we give our lives as a sacrifice and love is not in us, it does not count for anything.

We have read in the scriptures of the Bible that love is patient and kind and is not jealous or boastful. Love is not rude and does not seek out evil. Love thinks the very best of someone else. We also examined some of the life situations in which our Lord exhibited love and let the wisdom of God flow through Him—specifically, when confronted by people who wanted to find a reason to accuse Him of making a mistake in His teachings or trapping Him into breaking one of the laws of Moses. In this world we have limited knowledge and understanding.

Someday our Lord will return, and we will see truth and reality as it is. Have patience, my friend, that day is coming. In the meantime, our Lord has given us a charge to love Him and to love others as ourselves.

THE HOLY SPIRIT: GOD'S LOVE IN US

*J*esus did not leave us on our own. He gave us a helper. The eternal thread of love that comes from God to Jesus, His Son, now continues through the Holy Spirit who abides in us. We in turn communicate that love back to the Father, and as a result, God's perfect love has now come full circle. God's love has found a way. God has never stopped loving us. Even though sin separated God from mankind, God found a way for His perfect love, not only to reach us, but also to dwell within us. The cost was beyond our comprehension. God has made His love accessible to all who will receive it. The heavenly Father has made it possible for us to be a loving family again. Even death could not conquer this love. It has taken the complete Godhead (Father, Son, and Holy Spirit) to fulfill this desire of the Father. The Holy Spirit is God's love operating in us.

The Holy Spirit, like the rest of the Godhead, has always been in existence and is the third member of the Godhead. "And the Spirit of God was hovering over the face of the waters" (Genesis 1:2b, NKJ). The Holy Spirit was present in the days of Jesus and even involved in his birth. "Now the birth of Jesus Christ was as follows: After His mother Mary was betrothed to Joseph, before they came together, she was found with child of the Holy Spirit" (Matthew 1:18, NKJ). It is the Spirit that gave Mary the component of life within her. "It is the Spirit who gives life; the flesh profits nothing. The words that I speak to you are spirit, and they are life" (John 6:63, NKJ).

John the Baptist also had a miracle birth. In the following scripture, an angel of the Lord is talking to Zacharias (who would be John's father) and speaking of John and his ministry. "For He will be great in the sight of the Lord, and shall drink neither wine nor strong drink. He will also be filled with the Holy Spirit, even from his mother's womb" (Luke 1:15, NKJ). The Holy Spirit was at work in the earth and still is at work doing the will of the Father in worldly affairs as well as in individual lives. After Jesus left the earth to go to the Father, He sent the Holy Spirit to further help mankind. In the following scripture, Jesus explains the mission of the Holy Spirit while He is here on earth.

However, I am telling you nothing but the truth when I say, it is profitable—good, expedient advantageous—for you that I go away. Because if I do not go away, the Comforter (Counselor, Helper, Advocate, Intercessor, Strengthener, Standby) will not come to you—into close fellowship with you. But if I go away, I will send Him to you—to be in close fellowship with you. And when He comes, He will convict and convince the world and bring demonstration to it about sin and about righteousness—uprightness of heart and right standing with God—and about judgment. About sin, because they do not believe on Me—trust in, rely on and adhere to Me. About righteousness—uprightness of heart and right standing with God—because I go to My Father and you will see Me no longer. About judgment, because the ruler (prince) of this world (Satan) is judged and condemned and sentence already is passed upon him. I have still many things to say to you, but you are not able to bear them or to take them upon you or to grasp them now. But when He, the Spirit of Truth (the truth-giving Spirit) comes, He will guide you into all the truth—the whole, full truth. For He will not speak His own message—on His own authority—but He will tell whatever He hears [from the

Father, He will give the message that has been given to Him] and He will announce and declare to you the things that are to come—that will happen in the future He will honor and glorify Me, because He will take of (receive, draw upon) what is Mine and will reveal (declare, disclose, transmit) it to you. Everything that the Father has is Mine. That is what I meant when I said that He will take the things that are Mine and will reveal (declare, disclose, transmit) them to you.

—John 16:7-15 (Amplified)

This is a good scripture to tell us who the Holy Spirit is and what He was sent here to do for mankind. One of the first things Jesus tells us is that if He does not go away (to the Father) the Holy Spirit will not come to us in close fellowship. Jesus was a man, and even though He was part God, He was not omnipresent before His death and resurrection. This was made possible by the Holy Spirit. By the Spirit of God, Christ dwells in our hearts in close fellowship, being ever present. This is indeed a great advantage for us. He truly will never leave or forsake us because He is in us to help and guide us. Several names are given for the Holy Spirit, which also describes how He will assist us in our lives: Comforter, Counselor, Helper, Advocate, Intercessor, Strengthener, and

Standby. The Spirit will help us have victory in our lives, fulfill the will of God in the earth, and let the love of God flow through us to the Father and to others. The Holy Spirit is not here to take us over or make robots out of us. He will work with us and assist us to get the task done, whatever that task may be in our lives at the moment. He is going to help us make the right decisions and actions that will be in alignment with the will of the Father.

We still have choices to make. Many times I want the Holy Spirit to put some kind of whammy on me to get the job done, but He doesn't work that way. We are still in the driver's seat when it comes to making decisions for our lives. It boils down to listening to the advice of the still small voice of the Spirit of God and being obedient. Does any of this remind you of Adam and Eve in the Garden of Eden?

Jesus mentions in the above scripture that the Holy Spirit will convict the world of sin, righteousness, and judgment. The Holy Spirit will always be convicting the world of sin. We, as individuals, have a choice to yield to the convicting voice of the Holy Spirit, as do the people of this nation and in the world. When we don't live a life in alignment with the will of God, we can be led astray and begin to be deceived into the wrong thinking and wrong choices.

Jesus says that the Spirit of truth will guide us into all truth and that He will not speak on His own authority but will speak the words that the

Father has given Him. This sounds just like what Jesus said about Himself. "Do you not believe that I am in the Father, and the Father in Me? The words that I speak to you I do not speak on My own authority; but the Father who dwells in Me does the works" (John 14:10, NKJ). Jesus and the Holy Spirit speak the words that they hear from the Father. This is the Holy Trinity. They are separate, and yet they are one. They have a single purpose that is generated from the Father, and that is to do the will of God.

Likewise, since the Spirit of God dwells in us, shouldn't we also live to carry out the will of the Father? "Or do you not know that your body is the temple of the Holy Spirit who is in you, whom you have from God, and you are not your own? For you were bought at a price; therefore glorify God in your body and in your spirit, which are God's" (1 Corinthians 6:19-20, NKJ). If you are like me, our priorities in life could use some adjusting.

I owe the Holy Spirit an apology for not getting to know Him better and for not learning more about the work He is here to do in us. The Holy Spirit never draws attention to Himself. He is always pointing to the Father or to Jesus. Somehow it is easier to develop a relationship with the Father or Jesus because they are known as individuals and persons with emotions and feelings as we are. Even though they are also Spirit, it is easier to identify with the first two members of the Godhead for a relationship. There are plenty of pictures of Jesus with which we can relate, and we have the Bible that tells us of His life as a man. When I think of God, I picture a great arm reaching down from heaven or the Ancient of Days (God) sitting on a great throne while watching everything happen. In the case of the Holy Spirit, I picture in my mind a dove or a flash of white light. Perhaps it is because the Holy Spirit is indeed known mainly as a "Spirit" that His personality eludes us.

However, the Holy Spirit is a person and has a personality. He can be grieved. "And do not grieve the Holy Spirit of God, by whom you were sealed for the day of redemption" (Ephesians 4:30, NKJ). He can be lied to. "But Peter said, 'Ananias, why has Satan filled your heart to lie to the Holy Spirit and keep back part of the price of the land for yourself?'" (Acts 5:3, NKJ). He can also be blasphemed. Jesus is speaking in the following scripture.

> Assuredly, I say to you, all sins will be forgiven the sons of men, and whatever blasphemies they may utter; but He who blasphemes against the Holy Spirit never has forgiveness, but is subject to eternal condemnation because they said, He has an unclean spirit.

> —Mark 3:28-30 (NKJ)

The Spirit of God will show us the will of the Father. They are separate, and yet they are one. To miss out on understanding the purpose of the Holy Spirit in us, is to miss out on an important part of our relationship with the Godhead. My desire is to further identify the purpose of the Holy Spirit and the revelation of the love of God that He has come to reveal to us and in us. "Now hope does not disappoint, because the love of God has been poured out in our hearts by the Holy Spirit who was given to us" (Romans 5:5, NKJ). Perhaps we have missed out on a lot of victories in our lives by not understanding the complete work that the Holy Spirit was sent to do.

In the following scripture, Jesus is telling us that the Holy Spirit will bring all things to our remembrance.

> But the Comforter (Counselor, Helper, Intercessor, Advocate, Strengthener, Standby), the Holy Spirit, whom the Father will send in My name [in My place, to represent Me and act on My behalf], He will teach you all things. And He will cause you to recall—will remind you of, bring to your remembrance—everything I have told you.
>
> —John 14:26 (Amplified)

The Holy Spirit is here to help and counsel us, to teach us all things, as well as help our memories in recalling events, past teachings, and ideals or revelations of God stored in us for such a time as needed. "Now when they bring you to the synagogues and magistrates and authorities, do not worry about how or what you should answer, or what you should say. For the Holy Spirit will teach you in that very hour what you ought to say" (Luke 12:11-12, NKJ). As we yield to the Spirit of God, we have a divine, spiritual connection to the Father and Jesus. By the Holy Spirit of God, we have the mind of Christ to help give us an answer when needed. We must not forget that the Holy Spirit represents Jesus, acting on His instruction, and showing us the will of the heavenly Father. The relationship with the Holy Spirit is not to be taken lightly.

Jesus said because He was going to the Father we would do greater works than He did. "Most assuredly, I say to you, he who believes in Me, the works that I do he will do also; and greater works than these he will do, because I go to My Father" (John 14:12, NKJ). A lot of people think that this means that we will do greater miracles than Jesus did. I am not necessarily refuting this line of thought, but think about this. Jesus was one person preaching the gospel. When He ascended to the Father, one of the last commands Jesus gave to the disciples was to go into all the world and preach the gospel. This is our great commission as God's children. Jesus is speaking in this scripture.

> And He said to them, "Go into all the world and preach the gospel to every creature. He who believes and is baptized will be saved; but he who does not believe will be condemned. And these signs will follow those who believe: In My name they will cast out demons; they will speak with new tongues; they will take up serpents; and if they drink anything deadly, it will by no means hurt them; they will lay hands on the sick, and they will recover.

> —Mark 16:15-18 (NKJ)

This only confirms to us that God's heart is in saving souls and saving the lost. "For God so loved the world, that He gave His only begotten Son, that whoever believes in Him should not perish but have everlasting life" (John 3:16, NKJ). This is the first part of God's plan fulfilled since that day in the Garden of Eden when Adam and Eve gave into temptation. This act separated mankind from fellowship with God as well as mankind handing over dominion of the earth to Satan. Instead of eternal life, death came to all of God's creation. The heavenly Father has not deviated from His original plan in the Garden of Eden. God's plan will be complete when Jesus comes back and reigns as King of kings and Lord of lords over the earth. God will have His family and His creation back as He has always intended it to be.

If you want to know where God's heartbeat is, this is it. Notice that love is mentioned in this scripture. We can't seem to get away from it. God loved the world so much that He gave His Son as a sacrifice to save mankind. In developing a relationship with the Godhead, we realize that each has a part in our salvation and in our development of God's love in us. In doing this, we are fulfilling God's great commission and also fulfilling the commands of Jesus to love the Father and to love our neighbors as ourselves. If you think about it, they are both the same. If we love our Father and realize His desire, wouldn't it become our desire also? What better way to love our neighbor than to share the good news of the gospel in whatever way the Holy Spirit tells us. This also fulfills the will of the Father for us. Love God and love others.

The Holy Spirit's mission is also the same. The Spirit of God is not within us only to help us out of our individual problems, but there is an eternal purpose. In our relationship with the Holy Spirit, we must realize this and that the Spirit of God is here to do the Father's will and not just our own. We cannot order the Holy Spirit around or manipulate Him in any way. He will simply become silent to us.

Taking care of God's business in us and through us is what He wants to do. This boils down to choices! We have to let the Holy Spirit do the work in us for God's kingdom and for our individual lives that will bear fruit for the kingdom of God. The choice is ours in how we develop a relationship with the Spirit of God and yield our lives to Him that we may glorify God. The Holy Spirit of God within us is cleaning out the sin and darkness of our lives to make us more like Jesus convicting us of sin and unrighteousness. He is showing us the way and the truth of God if we will listen to Him. In short, He is helping us to work out our salvation and empowering us to do the will of God. "Work out your own salvation with fear and trembling; for it is God who works in you both to will and to do for His good pleasure" (Philippians 2:12b-13, NKJ). How is God working in you? How else but by the Holy Spirit? The Spirit reveals the love of God to us and in us to be given back to God and to give to others. This love, strength, wisdom, and counsel enables us to connect with our heavenly Father and tap into the His perfect love to give back to Him and others. It allows that perfect love to dwell in us for our own healing whether it is emotional or spiritual. To live a life in victory, we need to learn to draw upon the full benefits that the Spirit of God offers and wants to do within us. As a result, we are working in unity with the Father to fulfill our purpose in the kingdom of God. The Holy Spirit enables and empowers us within to successfully fulfill the plans of God for our lives.

Let's explore the leading of the Holy Spirit in the life of Jesus—our example. Jesus was baptized by John in the Jordan River. John the Baptist is speaking about Jesus in the following scripture.

> And John bore witness, saying, "I saw the Spirit descending from heaven like a dove, and He remained upon Him. I did not know Him, but He who sent me to baptize with water said to me, 'Upon whom you see the Spirit descending, and remaining on Him, this is He who baptizes with the Holy Spirit.' And I have seen and testified that this is the Son of God."
>
> —John 1:32-34 (NKJ)

This was no ordinary baptism for John. Something different happened that he had not seen before. John baptized with water, but afterward when Jesus came up out of the water, the heavenly Father filled Jesus with the Holy Spirit. Shortly after this event, The Holy Spirit led Jesus into the wilderness to be tempted by the devil. "Then Jesus, being filled with the Holy Spirit, returned from the Jordan and was led by the Spirit into the wilderness, being 'tempted' for forty days by the devil" (Luke 4:1-2a, NKJ).

The Spirit of God may lead us into places that we really do not want to go, but it is for our better outcome that He does. The Spirit is acting upon the orders of the Father. Jesus spoke of the anointing that enabled and empowered Him to do His ministry. He had gone to Nazareth on a Sabbath day, and upon entering a synagogue He was given the book of Isaiah to read.

> The Spirit of the Lord is upon Me, because He has anointed Me to preach the gospel to the poor; He has sent Me to heal the brokenhearted, to proclaim liberty to the captives and recovery of sight to the blind, to set at liberty those who are oppressed; to proclaim the acceptable year of the Lord." Then He closed the book, and gave it back to the attendant and sat down. And the eyes of all who were in the synagogue were fixed on Him. And he began to say to them, "Today this Scripture is fulfilled in your hearing."
>
> —Luke 4:18-21 (NKJ)

What Jesus was telling them was that He was the Messiah, and this scripture was about Him. Needless to say, His words were not received well, and they attempted to kill Him. He was saying the Spirit of the Lord was upon Him and He was anointed to do those things that were mentioned in the scripture. The Spirit of God enabled Jesus to do His ministry. In the following scripture Jesus says that even the casting out of demons was done by the Spirit of God. Jesus had just delivered a demon-possessed boy, and the Pharisees told the people that He did it by the power of Beelzebub (Satan).

> But Jesus knew their thoughts, and said to them: "Every kingdom divided against itself is brought to desolation, and every city or house divided against itself will not stand. If Satan casts out Satan, he is divided against himself. How then will his kingdom stand? And if I cast out demons by Beelzebub, by whom do your sons cast them out? Therefore they shall be your judges. But if I cast out demons by the Spirit of God, surely the kingdom of God has come upon you."
>
> —Matthew 12:25-28 (NKJ)

The work of the Holy Spirit is so important in God's eyes that He has given us boundaries concerning the Third Person in the Holy Trinity. This is a serious matter. Jesus gave us a solemn warning regarding the Spirit in the following scriptures. Jesus is speaking in these following scriptures.

> Therefore I tell you, every sin and blasphemy—that is, every evil, abusive, injurious speaking or indignity against sacred things—can be forgiven men, but

blasphemy against the (Holy) Spirit shall not and cannot be forgiven. And whoever speaks a word against the Son of man will be forgiven, but whoever speaks against the Spirit, the Holy One, will not be forgiven, either in this world and age or in the world and age to come.

—Matthew 12:31-32 (Amplified)

You may ask why Jesus would give us such a stern warning. We are able to speak against Jesus—but not the Holy Spirit? The work of the Holy Spirit is intimate, sacred, and a direct love connection between you and the Father. Remember, the Holy Spirit speaks for Jesus and the Father. The very Spirit of God dwells in us to commune, guide, direct, and help us to give true love and worship back to the Father. The Holy Spirit helps us be more like Jesus. This is no small gift that the Father has given us through Jesus Christ. This speaks of the intimacy that God has wanted from us since the beginning of time when we were created. As we yield to the Holy Spirit within us, we can communicate with Jesus, our High Priest, and to God. This is a very precious gift that God has given to us. Jesus paid a dear price to give the Holy Spirit to us and we must accept some responsibility in how we receive and acknowledge this precious gift.

What if someone who loves you gives you a gift that is valuable and precious to them? They had to make a sacrifice to be able to give you this gift. This person loves you totally and without reserve. What would happen if you threw the gift to the ground and declared it worthless? Can you imagine the pain, betrayal, and even the outrage that would be felt by the person who gave you the gift? We are responsible to the Creator and our Savior who has given us the gift of the Holy Spirit. Remember, the Holy Spirit is *holy*. We must treat this gift with great care and reverence. The Holy Spirit is a person and wants to develop a relationship with us. I am sure that I do not understand everything about the unpardonable sin that was mentioned earlier. The most that I can do is to give scripture in what the Bible says. If we truly love God from our heart, we don't have to worry about this sin that will not be forgiven. I have used Mark 3:29 previously in reference to the "unpardonable sin." Let's look at this scripture again using the Amplified Version.

> Truly and solemnly I say to you, all sins will be forgiven the so men, and whatever abusive and blasphemous things they utter; but whoever speaks abusively against or maliciously misrepresents the Holy Spirit can never get forgiveness, but is guilty of and is in the grasp of an everlasting trespass. For they persisted in saying, He has an unclean spirit.
>
> —Mark 3:28-30 (Amplified)

This scripture reveals a clue to what Jesus is saying about blasphemy. The people were saying that Jesus had an unclean spirit. This is a way of saying that the Holy Spirit that was within Jesus was evil. Jesus was trying to warn them of the error of their ways. These people had some very serious choices to make. We may not agree with what other Christians believe on doctrinal issues. One thing is for sure; as Christians, Jesus is our Lord and Savior, and the Holy Spirit dwells within us. We can all agree on that.

We are all in different places in our spiritual walk, but Jesus is Lord over all. Be very careful of the hasty words that we tend to utter when we hear a religious speaker or pastor and don't agree with the content of their words. Perhaps they are off in doctrine or thought. Christian groups who really love the Lord are known to disagree upon issues such as baptism or communion. People can make mistakes and not be right in all their thinking. No one is 100 percent correct in their thinking. The Spirit of God will always be in alignment with the Bible, which is God's Word. People must be given the benefit of the doubt when it comes to their "belief systems." Be wise and be kind toward other Christian groups. The revelation of God's Kingdom is being revealed to us daily. We will spend eternity learning the revelations that are hidden in the Bible for us. Let the Word of God and the Holy Spirit guide you. Watch the words that come out of your mouth. Don't be hasty to speak.

> And everyone who makes a statement or
> speaks a word against the Son of man, it will
> be forgiven him; but he who blasphemes
> against the Holy Spirit [that is, whoever
> intentionally comes short of the reverence
> due the Holy Spirit], it will not be forgiven
> him—for him there is no forgiveness."
>
> —Luke 12:10 (Amplified)

The Holy Spirit is here to help us and not to do us harm. He is here to do the work of the Father in us. Reverencing Him will honor the Father. There is a lot about the work of the Spirit that has yet to be discovered. While the time is given to us here on earth, let's ask the Holy Spirit to reveal Himself in a new and fresh way in our lives and to others.

The Holy Spirit executes the will of the Godhead and carries out the will of the Father just as Jesus does. He never draws attention to Himself. He is a person and can be grieved and lied to. (Do you know Him in each of these categories?) He will convict the world of sin, righteousness, and judgment. The Holy Spirit is God's gift of love to us. Because God is love, His Spirit is also love that has been imparted to us to help us overcome the roadblocks and obstacles in our lives. The Spirit of God also is still working in the world and will use us as instruments to get the gospel message out to all mankind. The Holy Spirit completes the cycle of God's love. It starts with the heavenly Father who is love and then is passed to Jesus who came to earth to show God's love and fulfill the plan of man's redemption.

Finally, when Jesus went to the Father after His resurrection, He sent the Holy Spirit to live and dwell in us. Just think of it! Perfect love dwelling in us to guide us into the perfect will of God. The Holy Spirit is in us to carry out the will of God and not our own will. The Spirit of God cannot be manipulated. We have to make the decision to be obedient to the leading of the Holy Spirit. The choice is ours just as Adam and Eve had to make the right choices. The work of the Holy Spirit is so important that Jesus said if we blaspheme the Father or Himself it could be forgiven, but if we blaspheme the Holy Spirit, we will not be forgiven. This tells us that the work of the Holy Spirit is not to be taken lightly.

To continue in examining the love of the Father, we will also continue the work of the Holy Spirit in us. Now is the time to start observing how the Lord, by His Spirit, helps us to overcome the roadblocks in our lives and fulfill His purpose. "And do not be conformed to this world, but be transformed by the renewing of your mind, that you may prove what is that good and acceptable and perfect will of God" (Romans 12:2, NKJ). It is the Holy Spirit that helps us to do this. He is in you to transform you into the image of Christ.

For those whom He foreknew—of whom
He was aware and loved beforehand—
He also destined from the beginning
(foreordaining them) to be molded into
the image of His Son [and share inwardly
His likeness], that He might become the
firstborn among many brethren, and
those whom He thus foreordained He
also called; and those whom He called, He
also justified—acquitted, made righteous,
putting them into right standing with
Himself. And those whom He justified, He
also glorified—raising them to a heavenly
dignity and condition [state of being].

—Romans 8:29-30 (Amplified)

This is done by the Spirit of God in us. The Holy
Spirit is a powerful gift from God to us. In the
following pages let's continue to learn how to
access and connect with the Spirit of God who is
in us to help, lead, and teach us the will of God in
our lives to live life in victory.

SUFFERING

*B*efore we go any further, we need to discuss the role of suffering in a believer's life. I can't count how many times I have raised my angry fist toward heaven and shouted to God, "If you love me, how can you stand by and watch me go through the unbearable, agonizing, and painful situations that happen in my life? Don't you care?" We look around at this degenerating planet and all the suffering, atrocities, and wrong doings, which are never brought into check. Why doesn't God do something? How can a God of love let these things continue and not react?

There was a time in my life that I had to admit to God that I did not want to serve a God that would allow any of His children to go through suffering. I suffered every day; why should I want more of the same? I didn't have the courage to sign up for more. God did not strike me with lightning. He held His peace and waited until I was ready to receive understanding of what the kingdom of God was about.

These are troublesome questions to answer, and yes God does have an answer in the Bible. God's plan for His children has not and will not change. It is essential for us to understand God's eternal plan because it helps us put things that are happening in our lives into perspective. Like putting together pieces of a puzzle, once all the pieces are in place, the whole puzzle can be seen in completion and understood for what it is.

From the beginning of creation, God has always wanted a family to live with Him in heaven. He created man and woman, put them in the Garden of Eden, and gave them access to everything with the exception of one tree. "And the Lord God commanded the man, saying, 'Of every tree of the garden you may freely eat; but of the tree of the knowledge of good and evil you shall not eat. For in the day that you eat of it you shall surely die'" (Genesis 2:16-17, NKJ). Adam and Eve chose to eat of the tree, and this is when suffering began for all mankind. This curse is still at work in the earth today as well as at work in every living being. God was not being cruel or unkind. God did not want or initiate suffering. Why doesn't God intervene more in earthly matters? Mankind, as a collective whole, made his choice, and God honored that choice. Death and suffering entered into the earth as a result of Adam's choice of disobedience.

Now each man and woman on earth must make life-and-death choices for each of their individual lives. We must understand that it is important to God that His children, of their own free will, make the right choices. We choose daily to live a life in obedience to God's principles and refusing sin, or we choose disobedience to God's principles and live according to our own will and principles. The consequences of sin and disobedience can bring suffering and tribulation. This brings pain to God's heart, as well. What parent wants to stand by and watch their child go through suffering, whether it is self-inflicted or not? Jesus told us that in this world we will have tribulation. "These things I have spoken to you, that in Me you may have peace. In the world you will have tribulation; but be of good cheer, I have overcome the world" (John 16:33, NKJ). Jesus was speaking to His followers as well as His enemies.

While we are alive on this earth, the war is on physically, spiritually, emotionally, and mentally. Suffering can come to us in many scenarios. Sometimes we suffer because we have done or said something wrong or failed to think before we act or speak. Sometimes trouble comes looking for us and we are just minding our own business. Some people are victims of an abuser from their early years. Whether it is from family, friends, work peers, or our enemies, trouble will come whether we initiate it or not. For some of us, pain and suffering have been our constant companions from childhood, and our tears flow every day without fail. It seems as if the pain will never end. I know what I am saying is not easy to hear. I am not speaking lightly of that pain, which you may still be carrying with you. Don't forget the hope Jesus left us in the last scripture we just read. Jesus told us to be "of good cheer" because He has overcome the world.

As long as there is sin and evil operating in the world, pain and suffering will abound. Suffering is a part of life down here. The devil is still on the loose and wreaking havoc. Everyone has a share, and yet some have more than others. As we have discussed earlier in this book, there will be a day when God will do something about the mess the world is in. He will return and make it all right. The evildoers will be punished, and the faithful will be rewarded. God does not take any pleasure in watching you or anyone else suffer. It pains His heart to see how mankind acts toward one another. People make the wrong choices and believe they can keep on going without any consequences. The good news is, for those who put their trust in God, they are not alone. "Have I not commanded you? Be strong and of good courage; do not be afraid, nor be dismayed, for the Lord your God is with you wherever you go" (Joshua 1:9, NKJ). God will never leave you or forsake you. God (Love) will never turn away from you or reject you. (Love) "bears all things, believes all things, hopes all things, endures all things. Love never fails." (1 Corinthians 13:7-8a, NKJ). Jesus came to heal the brokenhearted, and that means you and me.

> I have told you these things so that in Me you may have perfect peace and confidence. In the world you have tribulation and trials and distress and frustration; but be of good cheer—take courage, be confident, certain, undaunted—for I have overcome the world—I have deprived it of power to harm, have conquered it [for you].
>
> —John 16:33 (Amplified)

The good news is that the love of the Father is manifested in us by His giving us the gift of the Holy Spirit to dwell in us. Remember, one of the names of the Holy Spirit is the "Comforter." The Holy Spirit is in us to lead, guide, and direct us. Jesus is speaking in this scripture.

> However, I am telling you nothing but the truth when I say, it is profitable—good, expedient, advantageous—for you that I go away. Because if I do not go away, the Comforter (Counselor, Helper, Advocate, Intercessor, Strengthener, Standby) will not come to you—into close fellowship with

you. But if I go away, I will send Him to you—to be in close fellowship with you.

—John 16:7 (Amplified)

The Holy Spirit is here to counsel and to strengthen us through the times of suffering that we go through. This is an act, a gift of the Love of the Father to us. It is not the act of a cruel, abusive, or indifferent Father who doesn't care about His children.

The best example I can give of suffering would be in the life of Jesus. While on this earth, Jesus was part man as well as part God. While in the flesh, Jesus had to combat and overcome life issues, temptations, and trials just as any of us has to do. If this were not true, Jesus could not be our Savior. Jesus had choices just like we have. In the following scripture, the author is speaking of Jesus. "For we do not have a High Priest who cannot sympathize with our weaknesses, but was in all points tempted as we are, yet without sin" (Hebrews 4:15, NKJ). Like the rest of us, Jesus suffered in daily trials. Again in the following scripture, the author is speaking of Jesus.

Who, in the days of His flesh, when He had offered up prayers and supplications, with vehement cries and tears to Him who was able to save Him from death, and was heard because of His godly fear, though He

was a son, yet He learned obedience by the
things which He suffered. And having been
perfected, He became the author of eternal
salvation to all who obey Him.

—Hebrews 5:7-9 (NKJ)

I want to draw your attention to two issues
brought up in this scripture; Jesus learned
obedience by the things He suffered, and Jesus
was perfected by this suffering. I actually had to
read this scripture a couple of times. Jesus had to
learn obedience, and then He was perfected by
going through the suffering. When Jesus walked
in the flesh, he faced the pain, rejection, hurt,
anguish, and disappointments that this life on
earth brings. How did Jesus get victory over this
life? He submitted His will to that of His heavenly
Father. He understood the eternal plan of the
Father for His children. Jesus had a revelation of
the kingdom of God where one of the first and
foremost rules is to love God and then love others
as yourself. Remember, God is love. This is the
kind of love that fills heaven and the kind of love
that God wants us to obtain with the help of the
Spirit of God within us.

The following scripture is discussing part of the
definition of love. Love "bears all things, believes
all things, hopes all things, endures all things" (1
Corinthians 13:7, NKJ). All of us who know Jesus
as Lord and Savior have an eternal destiny. This

destiny surpasses the earthly bondages and pain that we know today. Because God is love and love endures all things, we can have hope in the love of God in us. "Now hope does not disappoint, because the love of God has been poured out in our hearts by the Holy Spirit who was given to us" (Romans 5:5, NKJ). It is the Holy Spirit in us who helps us make the right choices and get the victory that we need in our lives. As we yield to God's will in difficult times, Christ is being formed in us. Because He overcame the trials and sufferings that this world offered Him, we too can and will overcome the trials and sufferings that we face in this life. We are not alone.

Jesus had a revelation of the kingdom of God within Him. We need to look at suffering in a different context. We need to see the whole picture of what is happening around us. This is not easy to deal with when you are filled with pain, but please bear with me as we continue. The apostle Paul is speaking in the following scripture. "For I consider that the sufferings of this present time are not worthy to be compared with the glory which shall be revealed in us" (Romans 8:18, NKJ). Looking through the eyes of Jesus, and with the help of the Holy Spirit, we can face and endure suffering as Jesus did. Our heavenly Father has given us tools and knowledge to overcome this world. You do not have to hurt like you had before, and the pain will not be the same because our lives are hid in Christ. Let the Holy Spirit help you see beyond the pain you are feeling inside. Our faith in Jesus is our shield of defense against the darts of the enemy.

Suffering can also be used as a resistance that comes into our lives (in many forms) to make us stronger, or as we read in an earlier scripture, suffering will teach us obedience. Let's look at it this way; to keep fit, a person works out physically by exercising, riding a bike, swimming, participating in sports, etc. Most of the time in a physical workout, some pain can be felt.

Have you ever had anyone tell you about a sports injury? They know that even though there is pain involved, the outcome is going to be positive, resulting in a stronger, healthier body and a more pleasing physical appearance. An athlete does not focus on the pain that is endured. An athlete focuses on the results of the workout and the victory that it brings. For an athlete to have success, his physical body must face resistance and come into line (into submission) with the set goal.

If we choose not to work out and discipline our body, the opposite is true. Our body grows flabby, and the risk of having physical problems can increase within and without. This is also true in our spiritual walk concerning the suffering that we encounter. Consider it a spiritual exercise. Just as an athlete has to work out physically, spiritually we have to work out our salvation. We have to discipline our bodies and fleshly emotions to resist temptation and align with God's precepts, which make us strong enough to face and overcome the sufferings that we encounter in life.

Remember, love endures all things. How can you endure all things if there is nothing to endure? The love of God that resides in you has endured the pain and suffering from the beginning of time. God's love is not weak, and Jesus has proven it. He endured the cross and much more. Think about the suffering, rejection, and pain He suffered as a man. "For in that He Himself has suffered, being tempted, He is able to aid those who are tempted" (Hebrews 2:18, NKJ).

When temptation comes, the flesh suffers because of the struggle in the choices we must make as to whether we will yield or resist that temptation. (To give in to the flesh includes the desire to be angry, rebellious, drunk, lustful, etc.) Jesus, who has gone through all kinds of suffering, is able to help us by the Holy Spirit that He has put within all of us. You may ask, "What can I do about the pain that I am feeling right now?" You are in a love relationship with a loving God, and communication is essential. Right now, wherever you are, give that pain to Jesus and let Him take it from you. Tell Him what the pain is and how you are hurting and feeling. Ask for His help. He knows your heart and what you have been through as well as where you need to be emotionally, physically, and spiritually. Leave that pain, hurt, anger, and confusion at His feet.

Being led by the Holy Spirit, find scriptures in the Bible that will comfort and guide you through the issues that you are going through. It won't be easy, and at times you will want to take back the pain, but don't do it. When those feelings start to come your way, refuse to participate in the hurt. There is a real God out there who wants to help you. The following scripture is a prophecy spoken by a prophet, named Isaiah, about Jesus.

> He was despised and rejected and forsaken by men, a Man of sorrows and pains, and acquainted with grief and sickness; and as one from Whom men hide their faces He was despised, and we did not appreciate His worth or have any esteem for Him. Surely He has borne our griefs—sickness, weakness and distress—and carried our sorrows and pain [of punishment]. Yet we ignorantly considered Him stricken, smitten and afflicted by God [as with leprosy]. But He was wounded for our transgressions, He was bruised for our guilt and iniquities; the chastisement needful to obtain peace and well-being for us was upon Him, and with the stripes that wounded Him we are healed and made whole.

—Isaiah 53:3-5 (Amplified)

Jesus has taken on your grief and sorrow and obtained peace for you. Jesus was acquainted with grief and understands the pain and sorrow that you have endured. That means that you are not alone in any suffering that you are going through. Instead of focusing on the pain, you are now free to let the truth of God's Word fill you and set you free. This is done by reading and meditating on the words in the Bible, which are God's truth, not man's truth. Let the Holy Spirit lead you to the right scripture that fits your situation. It might be the "Love Chapter" in 1 Corinthians 13 or perhaps one of the Psalms. It may even be one of the Bible stories that you learned as a child.

As you read and meditate on the Word of God, it will become a strength and truth to your heart. There will be a struggle, no doubt. Your emotions and your mind will resist you all the way. It can, at times, seem like trying to paddle upstream without a paddle. But remember, just as the athlete has to persevere, so does the Christian in order to get a positive outcome.

Have you ever met a person that seemed to have a *perfect* life? They had material possessions, an attractive appearance, a successful boyfriend, girlfriend, or spouse, and not a care in the world? Their appearance is perfect, their dress is perfect, and not a hair on their head is out of place. Look a little closer, especially if they do not know the Lord as Savior. Do they seem a little shallow? Is there any depth to their personality? If a problem comes, can they handle it? What about their character or integrity?

It is the trials in our life that make us strong. When you seek counsel from someone, don't you look for someone who has had some experience in the pain or situation that you have had and can guide you in the right direction? We are here for one another. Sometimes we may go through a problem just so we can help someone else who is in the same situation.

We see suffering through the eyes of Jesus and use it for an eternal advantage as well as victory down here on earth. I know that for some us, the very thought of going through any more pain and sorrow is unbearable. We are not like the apostle Paul who learned to embrace his suffering and rejoice in it. Be ready to be taken to a higher level of understanding and perspective of the pain that you have experienced in the past as you begin to see your suffering through the eyes of Jesus. For some of us, the answer will not be what we are expecting. Are you ready to stop running and confront the suffering that stands in your way? Are you ready to gain more understanding of what God wants to do in your life to prepare you for His eternal kingdom? Each of us has to make the choice. What will yours be?

LOVE VERSUS FEAR

What are you afraid of? It could be anything from the big bully down the street to not having enough money to pay your bills. Let's not even mention the economy. How secure has your job been lately, or do you have a job? People are afraid, and yes some suffering is involved in being afraid. How many times have you lain awake at night while worrying about your family or having anxiety about what tomorrow may bring? People are afraid in their own homes. If an unfamiliar car is seen in the neighborhood, you can see the concern and fear in the faces of the people. They stop in their tracks to see if the person in the car can be recognized. Perhaps someone has come to burglarize a home or worse. In the flesh there are certainly plenty of reasons to fear, and yet should we? What does God say about fear?

In the following scripture, God is speaking to Joshua as he was getting ready to lead His chosen people from Egypt across the Jordan River into the land that God had promised them. "Have I not commanded you? Be strong and of good courage; do not be afraid, or dismayed, for the Lord your God is with you wherever you go" (Joshua 1:9, NKJ). The first thing we read in this scripture is that God is commanding Joshua to be strong and of good courage. The children of Israel were about to enter into battle with the strong tribes of people that already lived there as well as the giants of the land. There was much reason to fear. When God led His chosen people out of Egypt, the journey was not supposed to take very long. When they reached the edge of the promised land, the Lord told Moses to send out a man from each of the tribes to spy out the land of Canaan. Remember, in this situation God had already told the children of Israel that He would give them this land up front before they left Egypt. In spite of all the miracles they experienced just look at what happened next. "And the Lord spoke to Moses, saying, 'Send men to spy out the land of Canaan, which I am giving to the children of Israel; from each tribe of their fathers you shall send a man, every one a leader among them'" (Numbers 13:1-2, NKJ). So the men went out and spied on the inhabitants of the land and came back with their report.

Then they told him and said: "We went to the land where you sent us. It truly flows with milk and honey, and this is its fruit. Nevertheless the people who dwell in the land are strong; the cities are fortified and very large; moreover we saw the descendants of Anak there. The Amalekites dwell in the land of the south; the Hittites, the Jebusites, and the Amorites dwell in the mountains; and the Canaanites dwell by the sea and along the banks of the Jordan." Then Caleb quieted the people before Moses, and said, "Let us go up at once and take possession, for we are well able to overcome it." But the men who had gone up with him said, "We are not able to go up against the people, for they are stronger than we." And they gave the children of Israel a bad report of the land which they had spied out, saying, "The land through which we have gone as spies is a land that devours its inhabitants, and all the people whom we saw in it are men of great stature. There we saw the giants (the descendants of Anak came from the giants); and we were like grasshoppers in our own sight, and so we were in their sight."

—Numbers 13:27-33 (NKJ)

You can imagine the panic and fear that spread throughout the camp. The people started to complain of their situation.

> And all the children of Israel complained against Moses and Aaron, and the whole congregation said to them, "If only we had died in the land of Egypt! Or if only we had died in this wilderness! Why has the Lord brought us to this land to fall by the sword, that our wives and children should become victims? Would it not be better for us to return to Egypt?" So they said to one another, "Let us select a leader and return to Egypt."
>
> —Numbers 14:2-4 (NKJ)

Remember, the children of Israel were slaves in Egypt, and life was miserable, but they were acting like it was heaven compared to what the Lord had planned for them. They were looking at the situation with their natural eyes. God wanted them to have faith in Him just as He wants us to do today. This was rebellion, rejection toward God, and yes it was in the form of fear.

"Then the Lord said to Moses; 'How long will these people reject Me? And how long will they not believe Me, with all the signs which I have performed among them?'" (Numbers 14:11, NKJ) From this scripture, I realized just how personal

God took the unbelief and fear that was displayed by the spies that gave such a bad report. In God's eyes, this people rejected Him personally, and even with all of the miracles that He did among them, they still did not believe Him. After this, God threatened to destroy this people and start over. Moses interceded, and the Lord pardoned them, but they would pay for their wrong choices and rebellion against Him.

> Because all these men who have seen My glory and the signs which I did in Egypt and in the wilderness, and have put Me to the test now these ten times, and have not heeded My voice, they certainly shall not see the land of which I swore to their fathers, nor shall any of those who rejected Me see it. But my servant Caleb, because he has a different spirit in him and has followed Me fully, I will bring into the land where he went, and his descendants shall inherit it.

> —Numbers 14:22-24 (NKJ)

The children of Israel had been experiencing miracles every day. God provided manna for food every day for this people. Time after time He delivered them from their enemies and from being wiped out as a people, yet they were still afraid and rejected the Lord. They didn't reject the gifts or miracles; they rejected the giver, the Lord who wanted them to have faith in Him and trust Him as their deliverer.

We cannot take the love and grace of God lightly. It is a great honor to have the Lord speak to you and move in your life. We are responsible for the light or truth that we have. That is a great responsibility. Jesus is speaking in the following scripture. "For everyone to whom much is given, from him much will be required; and to whom much has been committed, of him they will ask the more" (Luke 12:48b, NKJ). The children of Israel had been given much. No other race of people on this earth had experienced more miracles than they did, and yet they would not believe that God could deliver them. This act of fear on their part delayed the blessing God wanted them to have, and in their fear they rejected God.

In this situation, fear brought serious consequences. The people chose to look at the natural situation (the giants and the strong people who dwelled in the land) instead of the God who had performed many miracles in order to give them this land flowing with milk and honey. God is faithful. He still planned to lead the people into the land, but they had to remain in the wilderness for forty years as a punishment for their rebellion. The generation that rejected Him would die in the wilderness, but the next generation would have another chance to make the right choice. God has patience, and He will never give up His plan for

His children. The following scripture describes the kind of love that God has for His children. Love "bears all things, believes all things, hopes all things, endures all things. Love never fails" (1 Corinthians 13:7-8a, NKJ).

Worry is a form of fear that is common in the day that we live in. There certainly is a lot to worry about if we focus on the natural things happening today. Families are dealing with unemployment, financial difficulty, healthcare, insurance, and those ever-rising utility and gas bills, and let's not forget the various rising taxes. For older citizens there is a concern about the future of Social Security, Medicare, and what the future will bring as incomes get more fixed and costs keep going up. The baby boomers are getting to be of retirement age, and the country is running out of money. But be of good cheer; you have a God who loves you and saw that times like this were coming. What God wants is for His people to have faith in Him. Have faith in the love that God has for you. In the time that Jesus was in the earth, there was much fear, and in the following scripture Jesus is comforting the people. His words are also for your comfort because His words are as true for today as they were back then.

> Therefore I say to you, do not worry about your life, what you will eat or what you will drink; nor about your body, what you will put on. Is not life more than food and the

body more than clothing? Look at the birds of the air, for they neither sow nor reap nor gather into barns; yet your heavenly Father feeds them. Are you not of more value than they? Which of you by worrying can add one cubit to his stature? So why do you worry about clothing? Consider the lilies of the field, how they grow; they neither toil nor spin; and yet I say to you that even Solomon in all his glory was not arrayed like one of these. Now if God so clothes the grass of the field, which today is, and tomorrow is thrown into the oven, will He not much more clothe you, O you of little faith? Therefore do not worry, saying, 'What shall we eat?' or 'What shall we drink?' or 'What shall we wear?' For after all these things the Gentiles seek. For your heavenly Father knows that you need all these things. But seek first the kingdom of God and His righteousness, and all these things shall be added to you. Therefore do not worry about tomorrow, for tomorrow will worry about its own things. Sufficient for the day is its own trouble.

—Matthew 6:25-34 (NKJ)

As Jesus preached the kingdom of God, He was showing us, by example and in His teachings, how to live and act as citizens of the kingdom of God even though we are currently living in a corrupt world. This was true back then as it is now. In this scripture Jesus is reasoning with the people in using everyday situations for His example. Eating, drinking, and having clothes to wear were an important part of life. Jesus also said that we have little faith when we worry.

I have to raise my hand and say, "Guilty," on that one. My first reaction to life's situation is to worry. Jesus told us that if we seek first the kingdom of God, all things would be added to us. And what does it mean to seek the kingdom of God? This is what this book has been about from the beginning. Making a choice of your own free will to love and obey God and to love and serve others.

> There is no fear in love—dread does not exist; but full-grown (complete, perfect) love turns fear out of doors and expels every trace of terror! For fear brings with it the thought of punishment, and (so) he who is afraid has not reached the full maturity of love—is not yet grown into love's complete perfection. We love Him, because He first loved us.
>
> —1John 4:18-19 (Amplified)

Remember, God is love. Once we get our priorities in God's order, He is free to move on our behalf. Fear can be a serious distraction, and our emotions can severely be affected. Fear can bring sickness, paranoia, and mental distress. When we are confronted with fear our first reaction should be to focus and have faith in the love that God, our heavenly Father, has for us. "For you did not receive the spirit of bondage again to fear, but you received the Spirit of adoption by whom we cry out, 'Abba, Father.' The Spirit Himself bears witness with our spirit that we are children of God" (Romans 8:15-16, NKJ). The Holy Spirit, God's gift of love to us, is in us to bear witness that we are God's children. Remember, one of the functions of the Holy Spirit is to help us in our weaknesses and be a strengthener to us. Therefore, we do not have to give in to fear. The following scripture only confirms God's desire for us not to fear.

> And do not fear those who kill the body but cannot kill the soul. But rather fear Him who is able to destroy both soul and body in hell. Are not two sparrows sold for a copper coin? And not one of them falls to the ground apart from your Father's will. But the very hairs of your head are all numbered. Do not fear therefore; you are of more value than many sparrows.
>
> —Matthew 10:28-31 (NKJ)

How can we learn to seek the kingdom of God rather that spend all our time just worrying about how we are going to get through the day? How will the Holy Spirit, God's gift of love to and in us, help us overcome fear and be made perfect in love? Have courage, children of God; we can do this!

We do know one thing for sure. God does not want us to be in fear in any given situation. There are many scriptures consisting of God and Jesus telling His people down through the ages not to be afraid. To be in fear is to be in great torment. Fear and love are opposites. To fear in a situation is to believe that God can't get us through the circumstances that are before us.

Consider the Bible story of Shadrach, Meshach, and Abednego in the furnace of fire. These three Hebrew children had, what some would consider, a difficult choice to make. King Nebuchadnezzar had a golden image made, and when a certain sound was made, the people were to bow down and worship the image. Whoever refused to obey this decree that the king had made would be cast into the furnace of fire. Shadrach, Meshach, and Abednego refused to worship the golden image. When they were brought before the king and asked to account for their actions, the three Hebrew children replied as in the following scripture.

> Shadrach, Meshach, and Abed-Nego answered and said to the king, "O Nebuchadnezzar, we have no need to answer you in this matter. If that is the case, our God whom we serve is able to deliver

> us from the burning fiery furnace, and He
> will deliver us from your hand, O king. But
> if not, let it be known to you, O king, that
> we do not serve your gods, nor will we
> worship the gold image which you have
> set up."
>
> —Daniel 3:16-18 (NKJ)

The king was filled with anger at this response and had the furnace heated up seven times more than normal. The three Hebrew children were thrown into the furnace, not knowing what their fate would be. They acknowledged that God could save them in this situation, but even if He didn't, they would still not bow down to the golden image. They made this choice of their own free will, putting their lives at risk for their faith. This could have been an occasion to fear. It doesn't say in the Bible if fear was a factor for these three young men. They totally put their lives in the hands of the living God. Their fate was up to the Creator.

> Then King Nebuchadnezzar was
> astonished; and he rose in haste and spoke,
> saying to his counselors, "Did we not cast
> three men bound into the midst of the fire?"
> They answered and said to the king, "True,
> O king." "Look!" he answered, "I see four
> men loose, walking in the midst of the
> fire; and they are not hurt, and the form

of the fourth is like the Son of God." Then Nebuchadnezzar went near the mouth of the burning fiery furnace and spoke, saying, "Shadrach, Meshach, and Abed-Nego, servants of the Most High God, come out and come here." Then Shadrach, Meshach, and Abed-Nego came from the midst of the fire. And the satraps, administrators, governors, and the king's counselors gathered together, and they saw these men on whose bodies the fire had no power; the hair of their head was not singed nor were their garments affected, and the smell of fire was not on them.

—Daniel 3:24-27 (NKJ)

The point of this story is that these three young men made a choice not to bow down to another God. In the physical realm, God did deliver them. However, they well knew that even if they had died, their souls were eternal, and they still would have won by gaining eternal life. They trusted and believed in the God they served. What do these young men have that we need to be able to face our fears? They had faith and trust in God, not just in the intellect but in their heart. They were ready to put their lives on the line for what they believed. Their relationship with God was real.

Do you love God? "And now abide faith, hope, love, these three; but the greatest of these is love" (1

Corinthians 13:13, nkj). In order to love someone, trust and faith is an important ingredient in a love relationship. God wants us to trust, hope, believe, and have faith that what He says is true. Our own nature opposes this concept. Our fleshly nature tends to look at the natural and factual evidence and wants to respond accordingly to what the physical realm offers.

When we are focusing only on the natural realm, fear is usually the end result. However, there is a spiritual realm that is just as real as the physical realm, and that is where God is and where the kingdom of God exists. Jesus tells us several times in the Bible not to consider the natural realm but see the reality of the spiritual realm. Our body is made up of flesh that will perish, but in us is a spiritual component (human spirit) that is eternal. Even though we are in the world, we are not of the world. Jesus is speaking in the following scripture. "If the world hates you, you know that it hated Me before it hated you. If you were of the world, the world would love its own. Yet because you are not of the world, but I chose you out of the world, therefore the world hates you" (John 15:18-19, nkj).

The kingdom of God will not be established here on earth physically until Jesus comes back to set up His spiritual headquarters in Jerusalem. His kingdom is in heaven, and that is why Jesus wants us to think outside of the natural realm and more in the spiritual realm. This is where our victory lies. In the following scripture, Jesus is being questioned by Pilate, and Pilate asked Jesus if He thought Himself to be the "King of the Jews."

"Jesus answered, 'My kingdom is not of this world. If My kingdom were of this world, My servants would fight, so that I should not be delivered to the Jews; but now my kingdom is not from here'" (John 18:36, NKJ). This is where faith comes in. The kingdom of God cannot be seen with the physical eyes but can be seen with the spiritual eyes. This unseen world must become as real as our own physical realm is to us. It is by faith that we overcome the fear in our lives.

> Now faith is the assurance (the confirmation, the title-deed) of the things [we] hope for, being the proof of things [we] do not see and the conviction of their reality—faith perceiving as real fact what is not revealed to the senses. For by [faith], and trust and holy fervor born of faith, the men of old had divine testimony borne to them and obtained a good report. By faith we understand that the worlds [during the successive ages] were framed—fashioned, put in order and equipped for their intended purpose—by the word of God, so that what we see was not made out of things which are visible.
>
> —Hebrews 11:1-3 (Amplified)

We have a love relationship with our heavenly Father, and our faith is the expression of the confidence and trust that we have in God. Is it possible to have love without trust? "But without faith it is impossible to please and be satisfactory to Him. For whoever would come near to God must (necessarily) believe that God exists and that He is the Rewarder of those who earnestly and diligently seek Him (out)" (Hebrews 11:6, Amplified). When we exhibit faith, we are demonstrating our love and trust in God and His Word regardless of what the physical evidence says.

Did you know that we have to fight for our faith? "Fight the good fight of faith, lay hold on eternal life, to which you were also called and have confessed the good confession in the presence of many witnesses" (1 Timothy 6:12, NKJ). So if we are fighting for faith, who is the enemy that we are fighting? I am glad you asked that question. We have already learned that the demonic realm led by Satan is our enemy always trying to block our faith and separate us from God. Jesus is speaking about the devil and his army in the following scripture. "The thief does not come except to steal, and to kill, and to destroy. I have come that they may have life, and that they may have it more abundantly" (John 10:10, NKJ).

The devil will often try to use fear as a weapon against the body of Christ. Fear distorts and weakens us while love builds us up and strengthens us, drawing us closer to God. Another enemy that we must contend with is our own flesh—the part of us that only wants to respond to the evidence that we can only see and touch in the physical realm. Sometimes we can be our own worst enemy. Our fleshly nature (mind, will, emotions) can be very strong in convincing us that God will not be there for us. It is like trying to paddle upstream without a paddle. Everything in your senses is saying, "God will not or cannot move in this situation."

Remember in Hebrews 11, it stated that faith perceives as a real fact what is not revealed to the senses. For example, when a financial crisis comes, or perhaps your employment situation is in jeopardy, what is your first reaction? Have you ever tried to take a stand on God's Word and try not to fall apart, causing a mental meltdown? Every fiber in your being is crying out in fear. After a while, you may even get a headache. You begin to get thoughts of losing everything and living on the street. This is not to mention losing sleep at night. You start speaking out those famous verses to combat the thoughts hitting your mind. "And my God shall supply all your need according to His riches in glory by Christ Jesus" (Philippians 4:19, NKJ). But the thoughts that are contrary to the Word of God are bombarding your mind, and there is not peace.

The battle for your faith is on. We have to face our fears just as the children of Israel had to face their fear of going into the land that God had promised them. This is not a fun exercise, but it is a test of our faith. The world is full of these opportunities. Undoubtedly, the issue is to believe and be convinced in our heart that God's Word and love is true. He will not let us fall.

Without faith it is impossible to please God. It is important to God that we trust Him regardless of what the circumstances look like. You cannot have a love relationship with God or any person without trust. Can you trust God? Can God trust you? I am going to repeat a scripture because it bears repeating. I know that I am throwing a lot of scriptures at you, but it is God's Word that is anointed, so please bear with me. "There is not fear in love; but perfect love casts out fear, because fear involves torment. But he who fears has not been made perfect in love" (1 John 4:18, NKJ).

What this boils down to is a love issue. If and when we are in unbelief, fear, worry, or mistrust, we need to be made perfect in love. Believing and having faith in God and His love for you is the antidote for fear. To seek perfect love is to seek God. We are told in scripture to seek first the kingdom of God. In God's love there is no fear of anything this world can dish out.

> Then one them, a lawyer, asked Him a question, testing Him, and saying, "Teacher, which is the great commandment in the law? Jesus said to him, " 'You shall love the Lord your God with all your heart,

with all your soul, and with all your mind.'
This is the first and great commandment.
And the second is like it: 'You shall love
your neighbor as yourself.' On these two
commandments hang all the Law and the
Prophets."

—Matthew 22:35-40 (NKJ)

If we love God with all our heart, soul, and mind,
fear will have no foothold in us. Our emotional
realm as well as our heart will be convinced that
God's love and Word are true, and the natural
circumstances that we see are temporary. Fear
cannot move us because we have been perfected in
love. We are talking about a love relationship with
God. This is what our heavenly Father has wanted
from the human race, including us as individuals,
since the beginning of creation. It all boils down
to love. A successful love relationship takes some
time and effort. After all, God loves you, and He
will spend your entire lifetime drawing you into a
love relationship with Him. He is willing, but we
have to make the choice to have a love relationship
with our heavenly Father.

When you love someone, you spend time
with them. Every word they speak is important.
Love can transcend rational thinking as we know
it. Haven't you heard the expression that love
is blind? This statement has often been said in

the negative context. Let's put it in the positive perspective. If we are blind, we can't see the natural circumstances. We are too enveloped in our Lover's gaze. This can be a positive thing if we are looking beyond the natural circumstances and seeing with our heavenly Father's eyes in the realm of His kingdom.

Let me put this in a more spiritual language. Learn to love the God who created all things and loves you the most; yes, no one will ever love you like He does. We need to trust in that love to help us in our hour of weakness. Spend more time communicating with the heavenly Father. Pray more often—and just not about yourself. In prayer time, take a while to be quiet and listen, giving God a chance to talk to you. Ask God what His prayer requests are. Fill your mind with the heavenly Father's thoughts by reading and studying the Bible. Replace the fear with faith in the God who loves you. Read the Bible because it is the inspired Word of God and shows us what His will is for us.

If one of your main issues is fear, just look up in the Bible how many times Jesus told us not to fear. Those scriptures are and can be a great comfort. Listen to the voice of the Holy Spirit that is within you. Remember, He is our Strengthener and Comforter. He will show you what to do in times of fear, and He knows what you need to do to strengthen your walk with God so that you can be closer to Him.

Yet to us God has unveiled and revealed them by and through His Spirit, for the Holy Spirit (Holy) Spirit searches diligently, exploring and examining everything, even sounding the profound and bottomless things of God—the divine counsels and things hidden and beyond man's scrutiny. For what person perceives (knows and understands) what passes through a man's thoughts except the man's own spirit within him? Just so no one discerns (comes to know and comprehend) the thoughts of God except the Spirit of God. Now we have not received the spirit (that belongs to) the world, but the (Holy) Spirit Who is from God, [given to us] that we might realize and comprehend and appreciate the gifts (of divine favor and blessing so freely and lavishly) bestowed on us by God.

—1 Corinthians 2:10-12 (Amplified)

The very counsel of God is within us in the form of the Holy Spirit. God has held nothing back from us. In the love of God, whom or what is there to fear? Yet we *do* fear. Faith and trust is not an easy road to take, but it is the right one. Love will always find a way. The love of God is the answer to all our fears. It is the strongest force in heaven and earth. "And now abide faith, hope, love, these three; but the greatest of these is love" (1 Corinthians 13:13, NKJ).

There is another kind of fear that we need to discuss. This is a fear of God. It is not the same kind of fear. To fear God is to show respect or reverence to God. "Only fear the Lord, and serve Him in truth with all your heart; for consider what great things He has done for you" (1 Samuel 12:24, NKJ). The Lord does not want us to be scared of Him—just the opposite. However, we do owe Him respect and reverence as our God and Creator. We should never forget our place before Him. Jesus did come down to earth on our level as a man but the result of the cross was that we would be raised up to His level to reign with Him in heaven. "You who fear the Lord, trust in the Lord; He is their help and their shield" (Psalm 115:11, NKJ). The following is another encouraging verse regarding the fear of the Lord. "O fear the Lord, you His saints! There is no want to those who fear Him" (Psalm 34:9, NKJ). The fear of God is part of your love relationship with Him. It is to Him that we yield our heart and soul. When you gave your life to Christ, you probably asked Him to be Lord over your life. We tend to forget these vows we make, but God doesn't forget.

In reviewing this chapter, we find that because of fear the children of Israel refused to go into the Promised Land and blamed God for the problem. The Lord took this situation as a sign of unbelief and rejection of Him. As a result the children of Israel had to wander in the desert for forty years until all the unbelievers died because that

GLENDA HAINES

generation would not be allowed to go into the promised land.

Jesus told us specifically not to worry about what we eat, drink, or even what clothes to wear. He said our heavenly Father knows we need these things and will supply them. If God takes care of the birds of the air, He will take care of us. Jesus said not to worry about tomorrow but to seek the kingdom of God and all things would be added to us. Jesus also said that to worry is to have little faith. To have fear is to need to be perfected or to mature in love. Since God's love is in us, we do not have to fear. Our flesh, which includes our mind, will, and emotions, sees the natural circumstances, and fear kicks in and takes us to panic mode. However, faith sees beyond the natural circumstances and believes the things of God.

In the story of Shadrach, Meshach, and Abednego, we saw three Hebrew children who had faith in God to the very point of death. When faced with the choice of bowing down to a false image or being faithful to God, they did not hesitate to choose God. The king had them thrown into a furnace of fire and God saved them. They did not know that God was going to save them; they were ready to die if necessary. They believed in God more than the circumstances before them. These three Hebrew children had faith to look beyond the visible circumstances and believe, trust, and have confidence in God. Will you believe what God is saying about your particular situation or what the circumstances are revealing? The choice will be yours.

Faith will go against what the natural senses are telling you. The battle will rage within you. Take courage; God has not left us alone without help or comfort. The very love of God is within us and the Holy Spirit has been given to us for strength and guidance. We need to develop the love relationship with our heavenly Father. As we grow in this perfect love that the Father has given us, we will begin to trust, believe, and have more faith in what His Word says. Our heart will be convinced, and our soul will yield itself to the truth of God's Word versus the natural circumstances. Again, we have choices to make. No one will ever love you like God does. Begin to spend more time with Him and listen to what the Holy Spirit is showing you to do. God has the answer for you that will bring you victory over the fears in your life.

LOVE VERSUS THE FLESH

So far, "making choices" seems to be the underlying theme. Adam and Eve had to make a choice as to whether they would eat from the tree of the knowledge of good and evil. God had to make choices not only in the making of creation and the earth but of what to do about the sin problem that Adam and Eve had made by eating the fruit from the forbidden tree. Jesus had to make choices as He walked here on this planet. Every day in our own personal lives we make lots of choices: what and how much to eat for our meals, what to wear, when and how to get to a destination, and how we choose to respond to the environment or circumstances that come our way. Even when we don't make a choice, we have chosen not to choose.

Some choices we make each day seem insignificant (which toothpaste to use), and some of our choices are automatic (driving to work every day the same way or taking the bus). On the other hand, some of the choices we make daily can be detrimental to our physical and emotional being (deciding to drive through a yellow or red light. In one second your life could change. The same thing can happen in our choices of relationships. A wrong or hasty word spoken can alter a relationship forever or even cause a job situation or a professional career to take a sudden turn for the worse.

On the other hand, the opposite is true. If we make a right decision or speak the right word in a given situation, we can be blessed in that circumstance. We make long—or short-term decisions on a regular basis, and as a result we live by the decisions that we make. We decide whether or not to go to college (money plays a big part in that decision), and we decide if we will marry the person who is in our lives or remain single. We decide what we will do with our free time and how we will spend our spare moments. We make a lot of decisions based on our material and physical surroundings in accordance with our comfort levels. To a point, we can choose the kind of friends that we have. Regardless of their social status, are they good friends or evil company? What kinds of choices have you made in your life, and have you been pleased with the results? We have the power within us to make good or bad decisions.

Within those decisions that we make each day, we are also making decisions that make an impact on our spiritual state. Good decisions can bring the blessings of God in our lives while bad or evil decisions could open up doors of lost opportunity that could be a deterrent to our spiritual and physical walk. In the following scripture, God is talking to the children of Israel. "I call Heaven and earth as witnesses today against you, that I have set before you life and death, the blessing and curse; therefore choose life, that both you and your descendants may live" (Deuteronomy 30:19, NKJ).

Living life is about choices. It is important to God that we, of our own free will, choose to follow after Him and accept His commandments, which brings life and blessing to us. The choice is ours. If we choose not to serve God, we will not be forced into obedience. The very God in heaven with all of His power will not stop us. Remember, God did not even stop Satan from rebellion in heaven. He made his choice, and look at the mess he is in now. He has brought misery upon the earth because of his arrogance, pride, and rebellion. The devil will have his day of judgment. The good news is that we still have a chance to make the right choices and align ourselves with the kingdom of God. The devil's fate is sealed. We can still act and make a difference. Today is the day to turn things around.

Joshua is speaking to the children of Israel in the following scripture.

> And if it seems evil to you to serve the Lord, choose for yourselves this day whom you will serve, whether the gods which your father served that were on the other side of the River, or the gods of the Amorites, in whose land you dwell. But as for me and my house, we will serve the Lord!
>
> —Joshua 24:15 (NKJ)

The first thing when you get up in the morning, make the most important decision you can make. No matter how many decisions that you are going to make, no matter how great or small, choose to serve God in all that you do. What has making the right decisions have to do in dealing with the flesh? I am glad you asked that question. The answer is *everything*. When it comes to the sins of the flesh, it is us (ourselves) who need to choose to yield to righteousness. In fighting the desires of the flesh, the choices we make are a key factor. The apostle Paul is speaking in the following scripture.

> I appeal to you therefore, brethren, and beg of you in view of [all] the mercies of God, to make a decisive dedication of your bodies—presenting all your members

and faculties—as a living sacrifice, holy (devoted, consecrated) and well pleasing to God, which is your reasonable (rational, intelligent) service and spiritual worship. Do not be conformed to this world— this age, fashioned after and adapted to its external, superficial customs. But be transformed (changed) by the [entire] renewal of your mind—by its ideals and its new attitude—so that you may prove [for yourselves] what is the good and acceptable and perfect will of God, even the thing which is good and acceptable and perfect [in His sight for you].

—Romans 12:1-2 (Amplified)

As you can see from our reading, this must be a decision of our own free will to serve God by yielding and presenting our bodies as a living sacrifice to God. As a living sacrifice, we put aside our own desires and plans to align and live our lives according to God's will.

Believe it or not, if you have accepted Jesus as Lord and Savior, you have already taken the most important step in making the right choice of overcoming the flesh. "I have been crucified with Christ; it is not longer I who live, but Christ lives in me; and the life which I now live in the flesh I live by faith in the Son of God, who loved me and gave Himself for me" (Galatians 2:20, NKJ). When we accepted Jesus as our Savior, we gave up our own initial rights and confessed Jesus as Lord over our lives. We are no longer in control. How quickly we forget the vow we made to Him by taking back our lives and making a mess of things. Our bodies house the very presence of God in the form of the Holy Spirit. This transformation took place when we made the eternal decision to give our lives to Jesus. At that time we committed to live for Him and not ourselves. Jesus bought our freedom from sin with the price of His own blood on the cross. It is up to us to keep that freedom by not yielding our bodies to the lusts or pleasures of the flesh.

The following scriptures are not all inclusive but can give us an understanding of what these sins involve. The apostle Paul is speaking here.

> If then you have been raised with Christ [to a new life, thus sharing His resurrection from the dead], aim at and seek the [rich, eternal treasures] that are above, where Christ is, seated at the right hand of God. And set your minds and keep them set on what is above—the higher things—not on the things that are on the earth. For [as far as this world is concerned] you have died, and your [new, real] life is hidden with Christ in God. When Christ Who is our life appears, then you also will appear with Him in (the splendor of His) glory. So kill (deaden, deprive of power) the evil desire

lurking in your members—those animal impulses and all that is earthly in you that is employed in sin: sexual vice, impurity, sensual appetites, unholy desires, and all greed and covetousness, for that is idolatry [the defying of self and other created things instead of God]. It is on account of these [very sins] that the [holy] anger of God is ever coming upon (those who are obstinately opposed to the divine will) the sons of disobedience. Among whom you also once walked, when you were living in and addicted to [such practices]. But now put away and rid yourselves [completely] of all these things: anger, rage, bad feeling toward others, curses and slander and foulmouthed abuse and shameful utterances from your lips! Do not lie to one another, for you have stripped off the old (unregenerate) self with its evil practices, and have clothed yourselves with the new [spiritual self], which is (ever in the process of being) renewed and remolded into (fuller and more perfect knowledge upon) knowledge, after the image (the likeness) of Him Who created it.

—Colossians 3:1-10 (Amplified)

We are to kill the evil desires within us. *We* are to put away all these sins of the flesh. It is up to each person to make the choice to put down the works of the flesh within themselves. Remember, the Holy Spirit is there to help us. We are not completely alone. The second thing I want to point out is that God did not give us a multiple choice in dealing with the sins of the flesh. The Lord didn't say that some of these sins were acceptable or that He would tolerate a little of each. The message is quite clear. Sin is sin, and we cannot whitewash or dilute it.

Some of the churches in this present day have been seduced into allowing sin to operate within the body of Christ, hoping not to offend anyone. This doesn't mean that we stop loving people and start judging everyone in our midst. We as members of the body of Christ have an obligation to each other. That obligation is love. We cannot turn a blind eye to sin. We have to help and pray for each other. Some of us get comfortable in the pew, and since we attend church on a regular basis, we think that God will allow some of our "little vices." After all, we are good people and don't harm anyone. To believe that is to deny the power of the Holy Spirit and the job He has been given by the heavenly Father to do in each of us— that job being to form the image of Christ in us.

What about the many Christians and others who come to church seeking help, deliverance, and compassion? How can the body of Christ even begin to minister to these hurting people if we are in denial that sin exists in our midst or that

God would even consider our unholy life styles and habits as sin? Some people think that God has changed His mind about His own Word. I think not! Think of all the kinds of addictions that are in the world and in the people that are sitting in the church today. People are too ashamed to seek help, and if they did, what would be our response...if we even knew *how* to respond? This is why we need the love of God in us. We all need help in some areas of the flesh, and we all need each other for strength and love. "For if you live according to the flesh you will die; but if by the Spirit you put to death the deeds of the body, you will live. For as many as are led by the Spirit of God, these are the sons of God" (Romans 8:13-14, NKJ). This scripture is the key to putting down the flesh. It is not by our own strength but by the Holy Spirit that we put to death the deeds of the body. God has showed His love for us by giving us the Holy Spirit to help us put down the flesh. Remember, no one is perfect. God is looking for a people whose heart is searching for Him. God knows our flesh is weak, and He wants to help us overcome these desires that stand as a barrier between us and Him. He is trying to bring us up to His level of righteousness, not be lowered down to our level of sin.

The actual list of sins in Colossians 3 are listed as follows (according to the Amplified Version): sexual vice, impurity, sensual appetites, unholy desires, all greed and covetousness, anger, rage, bad feeling toward others, curses, slander, foulmouthed abuse, shameful utterances from your lips, and lying to one another. The sins of the flesh are also listed in the book of Galatians. I am using the New King James Version this time. People have their favorite versions of the Bible, so I am doing both versions in order to help in clarifying some of the actions of the flesh.

> Now the works of the flesh are evident, which are adultery, fornication, uncleanness, lewdness, idolatry, sorcery, hatred, contentions, jealousies, outbursts of wrath, selfish ambitions, dissensions, heresies, envy, murders, drunkenness, revelries, and the like: of which I tell you beforehand, just as I also told you in time past, that those who practice such things will not inherit the kingdom of God.

> —Galatians 5:19-21 (NKJ)

Another item to add to this list would be our thought life. Sins of the flesh are not just limited to a physical action but to the very thoughts we have that come from within our heart. Jesus mentions this in the following scripture. "You have heard that it was said to those of old, 'You shall not commit adultery.' But I say to you that whoever looks at a woman to lust for her has already committed adultery with her in his heart" (Matthew 5:27-28, NKJ). Adultery is listed as a sin of the flesh, but even a lustful thought qualifies. Out of the heart come the issues of life. "For from within, out of the heart of men, proceed evil thoughts, adulteries, fornications, murders, thefts, covetousness, wickedness, deceit, lewdness, an evil eye, blasphemy, pride, foolishness. All these evil things come from within and defile a man" (Mark 7:21-23, NKJ). This list looks a lot like our listing of the sins of the flesh. Therefore, the sins of the flesh have a direct connection to the issues of our heart. No wonder, as we read in an earlier scripture, the Lord has commanded us to love Him with all our heart. All of us have a sin nature. Man acquired it in the Garden of Eden at the time of the fall of Adam and Eve. While we are alive on this planet, we have to put down this evil nature with its deeds and bring our soul under submission to the Lord Jesus Christ. Sin feels good to the flesh even if it may be just for a short time. After the sin, if our heart is not too hardened, what will often come are feelings of guilt and shame. This could be our own guilty conscience, or it could be the conviction of the Holy Spirit.

ANGER

Through the years, the pain and suffering that comes to each of us in so many different forms begins to take its toll. Each of us deals with pain in our own way. Some of us try to just ignore it and hope it will disappear, suppressing the hurt inside. Regardless of how we try, when direct action is not taken and we do not come to terms with our pain, anger and rage manifest themselves to release the buildup of the hurt within ourselves. A lot of times the anger gets directed to the wrong person. Have you ever heard of road rage? We end up taking our frustrations out on the first available object or person we see. Have you ever been going along in life one day and feel just fine and then all of a sudden out of nowhere you feel anger you cannot explain. You ask yourself, "Where did that come from?" Anger seeks revenge and unholy justice. You have been hurt, and now it is time to hurt someone and "get payback." We need to come to terms with our feelings and make peace. Understand yourself and the pain that is within you. The Holy Spirit is the best helper of all. He knows you inside and out. He can reveal the hidden things of your heart. All you have to do is ask and then be ready to listen to what He will show you. Paul wrote the words in the following scripture.

> When angry, do not sin; do not ever let your wrath—your exasperation, your fury or indignation—last until the sun goes down. Leave no [such] room or foothold for the devil—give no opportunity to him. Let the thief steal no more, but rather let him be industrious, making an honest living with

his own hands, so that he may be able to give to those in need.

—Ephesians 4:26-28 (Amplified)

The more you dwell on the problem, the angrier and more anxious you become. The flesh and its desires can be like a raging bull. In our anger we are giving the devil access to our lives. Anger does not contain forgiveness or any attribute of love, so the devil has a right to come into your life and steal whatever he can get. There is nothing God can do about it because you are the one who gave the devil the key to do what he wants. This can be an open door to the kind of suffering that God never intended for his children to bear. Just like Adam and Eve, we have made the choice.

Is our pain ever justified? God alone will have vengeance on the wicked. Sometimes the people who hurt us are just as ignorant about love and forgiveness as we are and need as much, if not more, help than we do. We all have a carnal nature (Adam-like nature, old nature, evil nature), and Jesus has set us free from ourselves by His work on the cross. It is up to us to be free and to choose freedom from anger. It will mean a struggle with the flesh. In the natural, your mind will not be able to comprehend what it means, choosing to love rather than to hate and be angry. Anger will burn within you and eat you up. Anger can cause you physical or mental harm and consume you to the point that you will miss all of the good things that are happening around you. "Make no friendship with an angry man, and with a furious man do not go, lest you learn his ways and set a snare for your soul" (Proverbs 22:24-25, NKJ).

An angry person is not very socially accepted. No matter how good your looks are, if you are angry, people tend to distance themselves from you. Joy and peace cannot abound where there is anger. An angry person cannot enjoy a healthy relationship with anyone, especially God. Jesus is speaking in this next scripture. "But I say to you who hear: Love your enemies, do good to those who hate you, bless those who curse you, and pray for those who spitefully use you" (Luke 6:27-28, NKJ). These are very hard words to hear. Isn't this the kind of love God has given you? When we hated Him, He chose to love us.

God didn't and doesn't hold a grudge against us after we have sinned or offended Him in some way. God hasn't told us that He never wants to see us again because we have offended Him. On the contrary, He is always ready to restore us back into His family. This is the kind of love God has given to us to give to others. Our heavenly Father knows how to heal your pain and give you peace. This is a part of having a relationship with a God who loves you and wants to give to you the secrets of the kingdom of heaven while here on earth. One of those secrets is how to love in a world of hate. The choice is yours. It is not too late. Make the right life choice and choose to love (with God's love), right now.

ADULTERY AND FORNICATION

I do not envy the young people of today having to face the seductions that are in the world that just lie in wait to trap and ensnare them. The media is full of sexual and seductive suggestions because "sex sells." You can hardly watch a TV show without immoral suggestions flooding the screen. The body of Christ has the responsibility to uphold and teach the commandments of God, including moral behavior. The Word of God is still true, and God hasn't changed his mind. Sex outside of marriage is not God's will for you. The flesh is strong, but with the help of the Holy Spirit within us, we are stronger. I encourage you to do what Joseph did in the Old Testament. After Joseph was taken to Egypt, he found favor with an officer of Pharaoh and was made the overseer of his house. The officer's wife wanted Joseph to commit adultery with her.

> And it came to pass after these things that his master's wife cast longing eyes on Joseph, and she said, "Lie with me." But he refused and said to his master's wife, "Look, my master does not know what is with me in the house and he has committed all that he has to my hand. There is no one

greater in this house than I, nor has he kept back anything from me but you, because you are his wife. How then can I do this great wickedness, and sin against God?" So it was, as she spoke to Joseph day by day, that he did not heed her to lie with her or to be with her. But it happened about this time, when Joseph went into the house to do his work, and none of the men of the house was inside, that she caught him by his garment, saying, "Lie with me." But he left his garment in her hand, and fled and ran outside.

—Genesis 39:7-12 (NKJ)

Joseph was in a bad situation, but he knew that this would be a sin before God and that he would be betraying the trust that his master had put in him. He chose to run away, literally, from the woman who was trying to seduce him. Note that Joseph didn't mention that he wasn't tempted or that she was too ugly. Joseph made a decision and stuck by it. In this story Joseph made the right decision, but the woman decided to make a false accusation (another sin of the flesh) and told everyone, including her husband, that Joseph mocked and insulted her. As a result, Joseph was put into prison. Eventually he was promoted to be second in command over Egypt. Because God was with him, many lives were saved from a famine that could have killed thousands, including his own family.

Sometimes when we make the right decision, it takes a while for things to get better. At first, things may get worse. When you take a stand to be celibate until marriage, you may, and probably will, be ridiculed and alienated for making that decision. I urge you to strengthen your relationship with the "Lover of your soul." He will help you. Moral discipline is not easy. Every hormone in your body is screaming out for relief. Jesus understands that our flesh is weak. The Lord gives us these commandments and teachings for a reason, not just to make us suffer.

> Do you not know that your bodies are members of Christ? Shall I then take the members of Christ and make them members of a harlot? Certainly not! Or do you not know that he who is joined to a harlot is one body with her? For "the two," He says, "shall become one flesh." But he who is joined to the Lord is one spirit with Him. Flee sexual immorality. Every sin that a man does is outside the body, but he who commits sexual immorality sins against his own body. Or do you not know that your body is the temple of the Holy Spirit who is in you, whom you have from God, and you are not your own? For you were bought

with a price; therefore glorify God in your body and in your spirit, which are God's.

—1 Corinthians 6:15-20 (NKJ)

In sexual intercourse, the two people become one flesh. It is not only a physical union but a spiritual one; therefore, to have sexual intercourse outside of marriage is a sin against your own body, which houses the Holy Spirit. It is defiling the temple of God. So there is a reason not to commit adultery or fornication. The good news is that God knows your heart and will forgive you if you repent and call upon Him. The heartbreak is that a lot of people, young and old, don't realize or recognize that adultery and fornication are a sin. If you are in this kind of situation, ask the Holy Spirit to reveal the truth to you, and remember that He is your Strengthener and Helper. Do not ignore or deny His counsel. He will not fail you. Be aware and be careful of the choices you make. God loves you, but He is still a Holy God, and His rules are the ones that really count. He loves you too much to turn a blind eye to a sin that can destroy your life and your soul.

SHAMEFUL UTTERANCES

Our mouth, left unguarded, can get us into a lot of trouble. In the following scripture Jesus is speaking to some of the religious leaders regarding the kingdom of God.

> Brood of vipers! How can you, being evil, speak good things? For out of the abundance of the heart the mouth speaks. A good man out of the good treasure of his heart brings forth good things, and an evil man out of the evil treasure brings forth evil things. But I say to you that for every idle word men may speak, they will give account of it in the day of judgment. For by your words you will be justified, and by your words you will be condemned.

> —Matthew 12:34-37 (NKJ)

Jesus is making it very clear that the words proceeding out of our mouths are truly coming from our hearts. Spoken words cannot be retracted. They are like arrows, and once released, the damage is done. All of us have been the victim of poorly chosen words at one time or another whether it has been delivered by a parent, friend, stranger, or enemy. Hurtful words pierce the heart like an arrow, and the pain is very real. Sometimes it is harder to recover from abusive words that are spoken than it is from a physical wound.

> Hide me from the secret plots of the wicked, from the rebellion of the workers

of iniquity, who sharpen their tongue like a sword, and bend their bows to shoot their arrows—bitter words, that they may shoot in secret at the blameless; suddenly they shoot at him and do not fear.

—Psalms 64:2-4 (NKJ)

There is a lot to be said about the words that we speak. Words are powerful, and God has a reason for commanding us to be careful about the words we speak. James, the brother of Jesus, is speaking in the following scripture.

Even so the tongue is a little member and boasts great things. See how great a forest a little fire kindles! And the tongue is a fire, a world of iniquity. The tongue is so set among our members that it defiles the whole body, and sets on fire the course of nature; and it is set on fire by hell. For every kind of beast and bird, of reptile and creature of the sea, is tamed and has been tamed by mankind. But no man can tame the tongue. It is an unruly evil, full of deadly poison. With it we bless our God and Father, and with it we curse men, who have been made in the similitude of God. Out of the same mouth proceed blessing and cursing. My Brethren, these things ought not to be so. Does a spring send forth fresh water and bitter from the same opening? Can a fig tree, my brethren, bear olives, or a grapevine bear figs? Thus no spring yields both salt water and fresh.

—James 3:5-12 (NKJ)

Our mouths were meant to bless God and speak the blessings of God, and yet we curse and bless with our tongue. It is almost like we have a split personality like Dr. Jekyll and Mr. Hyde. You can see the dilemma and confusion this can cause, especially if we call ourselves a "Christian." Don't get me wrong, Christians are not perfect but *are* forgiven. As God's children we are responsible to monitor our language the best that we can so that we can align our words with God's words. It is when we do this that our words will truly have power with the Father. I am not here to tell you just what words to speak or not to speak. I urge you to obey the Spirit of God within you. He is your Counselor. Choose your words wisely. Ask yourself if you are speaking blessings or curses. Are you telling the truth? Is your slang language acceptable to God? Are you speaking to others as you would like to be spoken to?

Our flesh needs to be brought into submission to the Holy Spirit. This is almost a moment-by-moment task each day of our lives. The apostle Paul said it clearly in the following scripture. "But

I discipline my body and bring it into subjection, lest when I have preached to others, I myself should become disqualified" (1 Corinthians 9:27, NKJ). We as God's children have to resist the thoughts and the emotions that come with suffering and temptation. God's ways are higher and His thoughts are higher than ours. Remember, He wants to bring us up to His level. Jesus has already come down to our level, won the war between good and evil for us, and reconciled us back to the heavenly Father. Our part in this war is to win as many battles with the flesh as we can and make the right choices, drawing closer to the heavenly Father. Making the right choices is what life is all about. Some of these choices will involve conflict and even suffering, but they are choices with eternal consequences and the reward is beyond belief when considering all that heaven will offer. The apostle Paul is speaking in the following scripture. This is a critical and key scripture that was given earlier in this chapter, and now I am going to use it again in the Amplified Version.

> For if you live according to [the dictates of] the flesh you will surely die. But if through the power of the (Holy) Spirit you are habitually putting to death—making extinct, deadening—the [evil] deeds prompted by the body, you shall [really

and genuinely] live forever. For all who are
led by the Spirit of God are sons of God.

—Romans 8:13-14 (Amplified)

I encourage you to be led by the Spirit of God.
Putting to death the deeds of the body is painful,
and yes there is suffering involved. Realize this
kind of suffering for what it is—an opportunity
to grow stronger and to overcome the flesh realm
that can hold you back from being the person that
God has called you to be. Your flesh does not want
you to mature spiritually. The flesh wants what
the flesh wants. The flesh is concerned about right
now and its own appetites for the present without
regard to the consequences or future of its action.
The flesh wants revenge, justice, and fleshly desires
fulfilled (if it feels good, do it). In other words, the
flesh desires to submit (by choice) to your mind,
will, and emotions without thought of others or
without regard to what the outcome might be.

Even though the war in the spirit realm has
been already won by Jesus, the battle still wages in
each of our hearts and will continue to do so until
we reach the end of our journey here on earth. The
apostle Paul is speaking in the following scripture.

For though we walk [live] in the flesh, we
are not carrying on our warfare according to
the flesh and using mere human weapons.
For the weapons of our warfare are not

physical [weapons of flesh and blood], but they are mighty before God for the overthrow and destruction of strongholds, [Inasmuch as we] refute arguments and theories and reasonings and every proud and lofty thing that sets itself up against the (true) knowledge of God; and we lead every thought and purpose away captive into the obedience of Christ, the Messiah, the Anointed One.

—2 Corinthians 10:3-5 (Amplified)

There are casualties all around us, and the "spiritual arrows" are flying everywhere. The pain is real, and some of the wounds we suffer are superficial while some go much deeper. Our battle may be as simple as turning off a television show that has sexual suggestions, walking away from the refrigerator, turning off the computer to pray, or putting down the cell phone to spend time with your family. The battle may be fierce, involving relationships and family members. Abusive family situations can run deep, and the scars that are left can last a lifetime if not brought into check. It takes the love of the heavenly Father to heal these wounds and scars.

Each day of our lives we make all kinds of decisions like what clothes to wear and what to eat at a meal. Some decisions are more important like how you will respond to someone who is unpleasant such as a driver in the car behind you that just honked his horn and yelled out an obscene word because you weren't driving like he thinks you should. Each person is responsible for his own actions before God. Life and all its consequences are a lot about the kinds of choices we make. In all the decisions we make, we need to consider God in the equation. It is important that we present our bodies as a living sacrifice, yielding our members to the Lord Jesus Christ. In this way the love of God has a chance to flow through us and reach a dying world in need of His love. Our lives are hidden in Christ, and it is not us who are living but Christ in us. Our lives are not our own.

When we accepted Jesus as Lord we asked Him to come into our hearts and be Lord over our lives, helping us to live a better life pleasing to God. This is done by the Holy Spirit in us who helps us overcome the deeds of the flesh. Our flesh is selfish, and being carnal wants to indulge and lust after what the world has to offer, thus exhibiting the emotional part of our nature that seeks its own selfish gratification. This is done with no regard to how other people are affected. Some of us have been abused or have experienced deep pain for many years. Our souls have been damaged, causing us to be unable to connect with others and leaving us unable to function socially. Feelings of anger and rejection make us defensive, causing us to build a wall around ourselves for protection so that no one can hurt us anymore. All of these are feelings that are of the flesh. Life is not fair. Pain and abuse make victims of all of us at one time or another. What happened to Jesus was far from fair. True love (the love of God), bears all things and suffers long. I am not talking about what is fair. I am talking about the kind of love that has always been and will ever be—a love that has no beginning and no end. This is the love that will win wars and make your enemies be at peace with you. This is the kind of love that will not depart from you but will last forever. This is the kind of love that can heal your deepest pain and sorrow. This is the kind of love that the Father has for you, and this is the kind of love that you can have within you to give to others.

We have just reviewed some of the actions of the flesh that come out of the heart, and they are evil thoughts, adulteries, fornications, murders, thefts, covetousness, wickedness, deceit, lewdness, an evil eye, blasphemy, pride, and foolishness. Because we are going against our own natural feelings in fighting the flesh, the pain and suffering that this can cause is very real. We choose to resist our natural feelings because there is a higher purpose to achieve other than our own immediate and temporary satisfaction. There is a higher source of love that wants to burst from us to touch others. God will not force us to give His love to others. We are free to act or react in the flesh if we desire. It is a struggle and a war raging daily within each of us. We are the ones who will determine the outcome by the choices we have made and by the choices we will make. Will our fleshly nature win out because we have given in and submitted ourselves to temptation? Or will the love of God that is in us win out as we yield ourselves to the Holy Spirit who helps us to overcome the deeds of the flesh? Jesus has won the war, but it is up to us to win the individual battles. The flesh is strong, and it is hard to resist its seductive power to fulfill its demands and desires.

There is no real justification for abuse or rejection among people. You would think that people would know better, but they don't. Please join me as we take a look at the "unforgiveness" that can dwell in people's hearts. In order for you to be truly free to receive the love and healing that God wants you to have, we must take this next part of our journey. God is with you, and He will never leave or forsake you. God's love has already made a way for you through Jesus Christ.

LOVE VERSUS UNFORGIVENESS

*W*hat can bring about or cause unforgiveness? When a person has been emotionally or physically wounded, our natural reaction is to strike back, demanding some kind of justice. Our flesh screams out for revenge. If someone has been the victim of a crime or has suffered long periods of physical or emotional abuse, the damage can last a lifetime. Betrayal, especially in a marriage for example, can be very traumatic. The very thought of a painful incident in our lives can bring immediate anger, fear, rage, torment, and even tears to our eyes. As a result, we try to bury the pain deep inside and may act out our anger and rage in our everyday life situations that are not even related to the problem. We might lash out at people without a cause or overreact in the most simple of situations. What we have done is to allow ourselves to become victims of our own circumstances. People can do horrible things to other people. We are angry and just don't know where to put all of that anger and injustice.

Do we have a right to be in pain? Do we have a right to demand justice in our situation? Many of us try to ignore our pain and bury it deep within ourselves, hoping it will go away. It never does unless we deal with it. Something wrong has happened to us, and we want God to do something about it. We have read in the Bible that Jesus wants us to forgive our enemies as well as our friends, family, and anyone else. How do we sidestep our pain, our emotional realm, and forgive others? Is God asking too much from us?

In the previous chapter, we learned that our emotional realm is a part of our flesh. This flesh lives and operates with a total focus on what is happening in the present. Our flesh wants what it wants. It reacts to the immediate feeling at the moment without any thought of the consequences or how others will be affected. Our flesh is selfish and only thinks about how *I* am feeling, or *I* need and deserve justice or even revenge right now. Everything operates around self and its needs. Our fleshly nature, which includes our mind, will, and emotions, needs to be brought under submission to the Holy Spirit that is residing within us. We cannot let our emotions be in control of our lives. The kingdom of God is based on serving and thinking about the needs of others rather than just serving our own needs (emotional and physical). We cannot let ourselves be consumed with thoughts of the pain and hurt we have had to endure. When we see to other people's needs, God takes care of our needs. It is the heavenly Father who heals our emotional, physical, and spiritual realm.

Forgiveness is the part of a relationship where God's love exists. Forgiveness is essential in any marriage relationship. Even among the best of friends, offenses can exist. In any healthy relationship, communication is the best road to forgiveness. If a friend has offended you, talk to him and express the fact that you have been hurt and do not appreciate that word, action, or attitude. Confront the situation as soon as possible so that the pain and hurt do not have time to fester and grow. It is like treating a physical wound; give it attention before it gets worse. The worst thing you can do is walk away and try to pretend that it didn't happen. For some of us, we just walk away and start shunning the offender, leaving the person wondering what they did that offended us. Give them a chance to ask forgiveness and have the relationship restored.

> Pay attention and always be on your guard—looking out for one another; If your brother sins (misses the mark), solemnly tell him so and reprove him, and if he repents (feels sorry for having sinned), forgive him. And even if he sins against you seven times

in a day, and turns to you seven times and says, I repent (I am sorry), you must forgive him—give up resentment and consider the offense as recalled and annulled.

—Luke 17:3-4 (Amplified)

It is sad to think of how many relationships are lost because of a lack of communication. God's love will reach out to remove the obstacles that stand in the way. The devil, the enemy of our soul, also comes to kill, steal, and destroy our relationship and fellowship with others and God. Our own selfish pride can also achieve the same destructive results. True love does not think evil. We need to give relationships a chance to grow and mature even through the hard times. Don't forget, there may come a time when you are on the other end of forgiveness and need forgiving. I know that when I have committed an offense and had not been aware of the situation that I would have liked the chance to say, "I am sorry. Please forgive me." No one likes confrontation, but give God's love a chance to work for the good regarding relationships with one another. No one is perfect, and all of us are going to make mistakes.

In His lifetime, Jesus had plenty of opportunities to hold unforgiveness or offense in His heart. In reading the gospels in the Bible, we find that people ridiculed Him, spat on Him, lied about Him, tried to stone Him, stole from Him (Judas was a thief and was in charge of their finances), and probably worst of all did not believe the words of His Father that He spoke to them. There were times that He was literally run out of town. Even His own family didn't believe Him. While on the cross He was totally alone. For an instant when He took on the sins of the world, even the Father turned His back and could not look on His only Son. Earlier within the last couple of chapters of this book, we read this scripture in Isaiah. It is a prophecy that speaks about Jesus.

> He was despised and rejected by men, a Man of sorrows and acquainted with grief. And we hid, as it were, our faces from Him; he was despised, and we did not esteem Him. Surely He has borne our griefs and carried our sorrows; yet we esteemed Him stricken, smitten by God and afflicted. But He was wounded for our transgressions, He was bruised for our iniquities; the chastisement of our peace was upon Him, and by His stripes we are healed.
>
> —Isaiah 53:3-5 (NKJ)

Jesus knows what your pain is all about. This is the same Jesus that has asked us to forgive our enemies and discard all injustices done to us. Jesus knows what He is talking about, and He is acquainted with your pain no matter how severe it is. This scripture says that Jesus has borne our grief, sickness, weakness, and anxiety as well as taken on the burden of our sorrow and pain. Jesus suffered in His life, also. He knows how to overcome, and He wants us to do the same. Jesus and the Father care for you and are touched by the pain you have had to bear. Please remember that Jesus also had to bear much pain in His life, and He chose to forgive rather than seek revenge upon His tormentors. This is the way of true love. Earlier in this book we discussed how bad things can happen to good people. Because sin is operating in this world, bad things will and are going to keep happening to people. This isn't what God wanted for us. Adam and Eve brought the curse of sin upon the earth and all mankind in the Garden of Eden. Sin will exist in the earth until Jesus comes back and sets everything back in order just the way the Father wanted it from the beginning. Jesus is speaking in the following scripture.

> I have told you these things so that in Me you may have perfect peace and confidence. In the world you have tribulation and trials and distress and frustration; but be of good cheer—take courage, be confident, certain, undaunted—for I have overcome the world.—I have deprived it of power to harm, have conquered it [for you].

> —John 16:33 (Amplified)

We are overcome by the Spirit of God that is within us. It is not the kind of overcoming that the flesh seeks after. This is how Jesus has overcome the world, not with justice or revenge but by the perfect love of God. The love of the Father is a higher kind of love than we have experienced here on earth. Earlier in this book we read in 1 Corinthians 13 the description of God's kind of love that describes not only the character of the Holy Trinity (God, Jesus, Holy Spirit), but it defines who God is (God is Love). Let me jog your memory and give you a few verses from this important chapter.

> Love suffers long and is kind; love does not envy; love does not parade itself, is not puffed up; does not behave rudely, does not seek its own, is not provoked, thinks no evil; does not rejoice in iniquity, but rejoices in the truth; bears all things, believes all things, hopes all things, endures all things.

> —1 Corinthians 13:4-7 (NKJ)

This is the kind of love that took Jesus to the cross that sets you free from your sins and translates you spiritually into God's kingdom. This is the same kind of love that the Father wants you to show to others and the world, the same kind of love that has been shown and given to you. This is what the kingdom of God is all about. Will you choose to show forth God's love today, or will you choose to respond to how you are treated by others? These are the choices that we make on a daily basis that count for eternity. Have you ever hurt someone or done something you wish that you hadn't? Do you want to be forgiven if you do a wrong? Shouldn't we be willing to forgive someone for their wrongful actions even if they have not asked forgiveness? This is exactly what Jesus did for us in our sinful condition. Jesus has forgiven us of our sins, and He wants us to forgive others when they sin against us. In the following scripture, Jesus is speaking.

> You have heard that it was said, "You shall love your neighbor and hate your enemy." But I say to you, love your enemies, bless those who curse you, do good to those who hate you, and pray for those who spitefully use you and persecute you, that you may be sons of your Father in heaven; for He makes His sun rise on the evil and on the good, and sends rain on the just and on the unjust.
>
> —Matthew 5:43-45 (NKJ)

We are to treat others as we would want them to treat us even when they don't treat us as we would like. This concept goes against every grain of our flesh. As well as being the right thing to do, it is a command of our heavenly Father. Never hesitate to ask the Holy Spirit to help you in this endeavor. The Holy Spirit helps us to overcome our flesh and will be there to strengthen you in your need for obedience to the will of the Father. The Apostle Paul wrote the following words.

> For you, brethren, have been called to liberty; only do not use liberty as an opportunity for the flesh, but through love serve one another. For all the law is fulfilled in one word, even in this: "You shall love your neighbor as yourself." But if you bite and devour one another, beware lest you be consumed by one another!

—Galatians 5:13-15 (NKJ)

You may be thinking that we are not under the "law," and this would not apply to us. Jesus mentioned this very subject. "Do not think that I came to destroy the Law or the Prophets. I did not come to destroy but to fulfill. For assuredly, I say to you, till heaven and earth pass away, one jot or one tittle will by no means pass from the law till all is fulfilled" (Matthew 5:17-18, NKJ). Christ has fulfilled the law with the love of the Father. We are also to fulfill the law with the love of God within us and flowing out from us to others. Earlier in this book we read that by loving God first and then loving our neighbor as ourselves we are fulfilling the law. This is what the kingdom of God is about.

I know that these are difficult words to hear and to comprehend, especially when you are a victim of abuse "emotionally or physically." Let me give you another example through the parable of the unforgiving servant whom Jesus spoke.

> Therefore the kingdom of heaven is like a human king who wished to settle accounts with his attendants. When he began the accounting, one was bought to him who owed him ten thousand talents [probably about $10,000,000], and because he could not pay, his master ordered him to be sold, with his wife and his children and everything that he possessed, and payment to be made. So the attendant fell on his knees, begging him, Have patience with me and I will pay you everything. And his master's heart was moved with compassion, and he released him and forgave him (cancelling) the debt. But that same attendant, as he went out, found one of his fellow attendants who owed him a hundred denarii [about twenty dollars]; and he caught him by the throat and said, pay what you owe! So his fellow attendant fell down and begged him earnestly, Give me time, and I will pay you all! But he was unwilling and went out and had him put in prison till he should pay the debt. When his fellow attendants saw what had happened,

they were greatly distressed, and they went and told everything that had taken place to their master. Then his master called him and said to him, You contemptible and wicked attendant! I forgave and cancelled all the [great] debt of yours because you begged me; and should you not have had pity and mercy on your fellow attendant, as I had pity and mercy on you? And in wrath his master turned him over to the torturers (the jailers), till he should pay all that he owed. So also My heavenly Father will deal with every one of you, if you do not freely forgive your brother from your heart his offenses.

—Matthew 18:23-35 (Amplified)

In this parable you have a man who was forgiven of a huge debt. This is not unlike the debt that we owed to God because of our sin. Sometimes we forget that we had our own sinful debt that Jesus did forgive. Sometimes we forget the price that Jesus paid on the cross in order to be able to forgive us of our sins. We, like the wicked servant, go out and refuse to give to someone else the mercy, compassion, and forgiveness that we have been given. The need for forgiveness doesn't stop at our salvation. We continually need to seek forgiveness of our heavenly Father, making forgiveness an ongoing "constant need" in our lives. As God is constantly forgiving us, we need to constantly be forgiving those who have offended us. Sin is sin no matter how big or small. We all have sinned, and because we are human we will continue to sin and need to continue to ask God to forgive us. The apostle John wrote the following words.

> But if we walk in the light as He is in the light, we have fellowship with one another, and the blood of Jesus Christ His Son cleanses us from all sin. If we say that we have no sin, we deceive ourselves, and the truth is not in us. If we confess our sins, he is faithful and just to forgive us our sins and to cleanse us from all unrighteousness. If we say that we have not sinned, we make Him a liar, and His word is not in us.
>
> —1 John 1:7-10 (NKJ)

We try to justify ourselves by saying, "I am a good person. I don't murder or steal. I might occasionally think unclean thoughts, give in to road rage once in a while, mutter some bad words on occasion, or tell a small, white lie on my income tax, but that certainly doesn't hurt anyone." We want to think that God may like us better because our sins are not as big or bad as other people's sins. Our sins aren't compared to one another but to the Word of God. Only God can judge our sins. Remember, He looks upon the heart and not just the outward actions that we do. Any sin is disobedience to God and demands accountability just like the king in the previous parable who was settling his accounts with his attendants. By the way, that day of settling accounts is coming for every person who has lived on this earth, and that includes you and me. Every one of us will have to give an account of our actions before the Lord. As difficult as this may sound, it is time for us to get our emotions into perspective align ourselves with the vision that God has for our lives. His plan for us goes beyond the pain that we are feeling at the moment or even the hurt that we have carried for years. We are dealing with eternal values as well as eternal consequences. As we have discussed earlier, Jesus can take that pain and heal our emotions if we will let Him. This frees us to be able to focus our thoughts on God's business and how we can fulfill His purpose in us and through us for the kingdom of God.

There is still another step that must be taken in the forgiving of others who have offended or hurt us whether it is justified or not. In the reading of the parable of the unforgiving servant, Jesus said that we need to forgive others from our heart. I want to mention this because I have rarely seen true forgiveness (from the heart) in the body of Christ, and I am not sure whether I have experienced this in my life. When God forgives someone, He restores them to Himself. When God forgives, He forgets. Our Lord does not file our sins away for future use. We can say we forgive someone with our lips, but our actions are far from it. Since we are Christians we are expected to forgive. Words flow from our mouth, but the offense remains in our heart, and our attitude and actions toward the offender remain un-forgiven. There is no restoration.

We may keep our distance from a person and the fellowship is broken because the pain, or memory of the pain, still remains. This is not true forgiveness. When the Lord says to forgive from your heart, this includes all that is you (mind, will, emotions). This is the type of forgiveness that God has given to you. Without the restoration, forgiveness is not complete. This may seem unreachable or impossible, but with God all things are possible. His Spirit (His love) is working in you and is helping you to do the Father's will. God would not ask us to do something that we can't do. God (Love) will find a way. God found a way for us by sending Jesus; therefore, He will find a way in your special situation to let the love of God flow and give you victory that you could never have dreamed of in this area. Forgiveness is the cornerstone and foundation of our salvation, and has a very high priority with God. You can be sure that if you ask the heavenly Father for help in the area of forgiveness, there will be a response. For such is the kingdom of heaven.

If I choose not to forgive others and hold on to my offense, are there any consequences that God warns me about? The answer is yes. The foundation of our salvation is based on forgiveness. Jesus forgave all of our past sins when we accepted Him as Lord and Savior. This forgiveness came at a huge price. Jesus went to the cross and became our sacrifice for the sins that we have committed and will, unfortunately, commit. Forgiveness did not end at the cross. We confess our sins before God to keep ourselves under the blood of Jesus and his righteousness. In turn, we are to forgive others. This is a direct command of God.

> For if you forgive people their trespasses— that is, their reckless and willful sins, leaving them, letting them go and giving up resentment—your heavenly Father will also forgive you. But if you do not forgive others their trespasses—their reckless and willful sins, leaving them, letting them go and giving up resentment—neither will your Father forgive you your trespasses.
>
> —Matthew 6:14-15 (Amplified)

Forgiveness is a very serious issue with the Father. It was serious enough that Jesus had to come down to earth as a man, overcome all temptation in the flesh, deal with everything that the devil could throw against Him, suffer unthinkable torture and pain, bear the emotional stress, humiliation, and physical pain that this world has to offer on a daily basis, and finally submit to being murdered. In the final act of all these atrocities, while right there on the cross, Jesus looked right at His killers and forgave them. "Then Jesus said, 'Father, forgive them, for they do not know what they do.' And they divided His garments and cast lots" (Luke 23:34, NKJ). This is where we need to have a fresh revelation of the price that was paid in order for us to be forgiven of our sins. If Jesus had to go through this kind of suffering, how much more important is it that we forgive others when they commit an offense against us? It is so important that our own salvation could depend on it. If we cannot forgive, we cannot be forgiven. Jesus is speaking in the following scripture. "And whenever you stand praying, if you have anything against anyone, forgive him, that your Father in heaven may also forgive you your trespasses. But if you do not forgive, neither will your Father in heaven forgive your trespasses" (Mark 11:25-26, NKJ). Forgiveness is the foundation of our faith. There is no salvation of mankind without the forgiveness of sins. Jesus bore our sins on the cross. Since Jesus forgave you of your sins, shouldn't you be able to forgive others of their sins as your heavenly Father would?

Unforgiveness affects not only ourselves but everyone around us. Choosing to forgive is a requirement in any successful relationship that we have. We are human beings and make mistakes. Too many times we utter words or do actions that we shouldn't without thinking of what their impact might be on other people. Offending people, whether on purpose or not, will happen to you as a part of life. Being offended will also happen as a part of life. You can't escape it. No one is going to act perfectly to everyone all the time. Sometimes people hurt people because they themselves, have been hurt, abused, or wounded, and do not know how to function in a normal relationship. People cannot give what they have not been given. An abuser cannot give love because they have no idea what love is. All they know is abuse. As a child of God, we have to look beyond our feelings and see through the eyes of Jesus. God's love goes beyond the flesh and feelings of the need for revenge. Remember, "Love bears all things." As God has forgiven us, He wants us to forgive others. God wants us to love others as we would want to be loved.

God's love also restores us back to Himself. God doesn't forgive us and then keep an account of our mistakes. This is not forgiveness. This is why God wants us to forgive others from our heart. We cannot forgive others verbally and still hold unforgiveness in our heart, treating them as our offenders and remembering the pain and hurt that they might have caused. True forgiveness means that you forgive a person from your heart, forget the incident, and restore them back to fellowship. For some of us, this can be done only as an act of faith to start with, but as we take that step of faith, God will help us. The Holy Spirit is there to strengthen and help us.

To choose not to forgive can have some grave consequences. The Lord tells us that if we do not forgive, then we will not be forgiven. These are hard words to hear, but think of how the Lord has freely forgiven all of our sins. He simply asks that we do the same. For such is the kingdom of God. Without forgiveness, there would be no salvation.

So far we have dealt with the enemies within ourselves—mainly our flesh. There is another enemy from without. This is the demonic realm and its agenda against your soul. The media of television has more shows concerning demons and their activity than ever before. A lot of theories abound about the demonic realm. Let's look at what the Bible says about the enemy of your soul so that you are armed with the truth for the battles that lie ahead.

LOVE VERSUS DEMONIC ACTIVITY

*T*he satanic realm includes angelic and demonic powers, all giving allegiance and service to the devil and his plan against God and His creation—man. At the beginning of this book, I discussed a little bit about Satan and who he is and his purpose regarding the kingdom of God. For us to better understand the attack of the devil and his army against God's people, we need to understand what the leader of this dark realm hopes to achieve by attacking our lives and why. God is speaking in the following scripture to Lucifer, who is also known as the devil, or Satan.

> You were the seal of perfection, full of wisdom and perfect in beauty. You were in Eden, the garden of God; every precious stone was your covering: The sardius,

topaz and diamond, beryl, onyx, and jasper, sapphire, turquoise and emerald with gold. The workmanship of your timbrels and pipes was prepared for you on the day you were created. You were the anointed cherub who covers; I established you; you were on the holy mountain of God; you walked back and forth in the midst of fiery stones. You were perfect in your ways from the day you were created, till iniquity was found in you. By the abundance of your trading you became filled with violence within, and you sinned; therefore I cast you as a profane thing out of the mountain of God; and I destroyed you, O covering cherub, from the midst of the fiery stones. Your heart was lifted up because of your beauty; you corrupted your wisdom for the sake of your splendor; I cast you to the ground, I laid you before kings, that they might gaze at you.

—Ezekiel 28:12b-17(NKJ)

Lucifer was on the holy mountain of God, which would be the location of God's throne. In this scripture, it is also mentioned that he was given workmanship of timbrels and pipes when he was created. He could have had a ministry in which he played a leadership role that involved praise and worship, which was special before God. He was called the "anointed" cherub. He was a cherub who "covers," and this suggests that he was in a position to protect or to guard something. It is interesting to note that cherubs were put on the mercy seat that sat on top of the Ark of the Covenant. The following scripture contains instructions God is giving Moses for the Ark of the Covenant (also called the Ark of Testimony).

> You shall make a mercy seat of pure gold; two and a half cubits shall be its length and a cubit and a half its width. And you shall make two cherubim of gold; of hammered work you shall make them at the two ends of the mercy seat. Make one cherub at one end, and the other cherub at the other end; you shall make the cherubim at the two ends of it of one piece with the mercy seat. And the cherubim shall stretch out their wings above, covering the mercy seat with their wings, and they shall face one another; the faces of the cherubim shall be toward the mercy seat. You shall put the mercy seat on top of the ark, and in the ark you shall put the Testimony that I will give you. And there I will meet with you, and I will speak with you from above the mercy seat, from between the two cherubim which are on the ark of the Testimony, about everything

which I will give you in commandment to
the children of Israel.

—Exodus 25:17-22 (NKJ)

Notice that the cherubim's wings "covered"
the mercy seat. Here we have the word *covered*
again, confirming that one of the duties of the
cherubs is to protect or guard. Above the mercy
seat and between the two cherubim God would
speak to Moses or one of the priests regarding the
children of Israel. If you look up the word *cherub*
in a concordance, you will find many references to
their ministry before God. Cherubs are mentioned
several times in the book of Ezekiel. In his visions,
Ezekiel saw cherubs ministering to God and
responding to His bidding. The point I am trying
to make is that the devil had a very important and
high position before God, and he chose to throw
it all away, becoming an enemy of our heavenly
Father. God wants us to serve him as a choice of
our own free will. Satan was given much and had
much responsibility. His beauty and talent were
unmatched, and this was a big part of his problem.
Pride began to dwell in his heart, and as we read
in Ezekiel 28, the devil was lifted up because of his
beauty. The following scripture describes Lucifer's
attitude that led to his expulsion from heaven.

How you are fallen from heaven, O Lucifer,
son of the morning! How you are cut down

to the ground, you who weakened the nations! For you have said in your heart: 'I will ascend into heaven, I will exalt my throne above the stars of God; I will also sit on the mount of the congregation on the farthest sides of the north; I will ascend above the heights of the clouds, I will be like the Most High.' Yet you shall be brought down to Sheol, to the lowest depths of the Pit.

—Isaiah 14:12-15 (NKJ)

You can definitely pick up the fact that Lucifer needed an attitude adjustment. He wanted to be like God, have a throne of his own, and be equal with God in every aspect. We have seen this in the earth on a lot smaller scale. Some people obtain a large amount of money or power, and all of a sudden the laws of the land do not apply to them because they consider themselves above the law.

Whenever we think of Satan, one of the first thoughts that comes to mind is the temptation and fall of Adam and Eve in the Garden of Eden. Eve was deceived from what God's original warning was to her and Adam about not eating the fruit of the tree. Satan twisted the words that God said and led Eve astray. Who wouldn't want to be like God? In tempting people to turn away from God, Satan and his army of demons and angels seduce, devour, and deceive the people of the earth. He wants God to fail in His plans for mankind and his goal is to turn and use God's very own creation (man) against Him. Jesus is referring to Satan as a thief in the following scripture. "The thief does not come except to steal, and to kill, and to destroy. I have come that they may have life, and that they may have it more abundantly" (John 10:10, NKJ). Satan and his army are not discriminating in whom they attack. The enemy of our soul attacks Christians and non-Christians.

The apostle Peter put it well in the following scripture. "Be sober, be vigilant; because your adversary the devil walks about like a roaring lion, seeking whom he may devour. Resist him, steadfast in the faith, knowing that the same sufferings are experienced by your brotherhood in the world" (1 Peter 5:8-9, NKJ). If you will notice, the word "sufferings" has been used in this scripture. The devil definitely has a lot to do with some but not all of the suffering of the world. He is the ultimate troublemaker, and he wants you to fail before God and man. He and his minions (demons and evil angels) are the ones that hinder and put roadblocks in your path. In his case, misery truly does love company. However, we do not have to be one of his victims. As the scripture has said, we need to be vigilant, aware of the enemy, and aware of the ways in which he comes to tempt us, with the potential to cause us to spiritually fall.

In the previous scripture, the devil is referred to as a roaring lion. This lion is looking for opportunity—an open door to walk through or a weakness that he can take advantage of. Temptation comes to people differently, depending upon the person and their weaknesses. The devil can and will use the weaknesses of the flesh and the lusts of the world to draw many into his snare. He will use anything to get our minds and focus off of the heavenly Father who loves us and can deliver us. As scripture has said, we can resist the devil, and that is what we have to do. I am about to give you some very good news in all of this. We do not have to become "dead meat" for the lion that is out to devour us. Just as the Father made a way for Jesus to rescue man from eternal death, He has made a way for us to have victory over the attack of the devil and his demons. "No temptation has overtaken you except such as is common to man; but God is faithful, who will not allow you to be tempted beyond what you are able, but with the temptation will also make the way of escape, that you may be able to bear it" (1 Corinthians 10:13, NKJ).

The devil or any demon in his army cannot just come in and take all you have and do whatever he wants. God has put a limit on him. Not only that, but the scripture says that God will make a way of escape for us, and that is good news. This doesn't mean that God is going to do all the work and we can just sit back and watch. Do you want to guess what our part is? You are right! We have to make the right choices in our lives that align with the will and precepts of God. Remember, if we seek first the kingdom of God, all things are added to us. This means that we must listen to the Holy Spirit within us. One of the names of the Holy Spirit is "Counselor." He is within us to show us the right way and is very good at giving us warning signs when danger is near. It is up to us to listen and follow the instructions that the Spirit gives us, and then we will have a way of escape. Don't forget that we can open the door to the devil to access our lives by committing sin and then, because of our disobedience, he has an avenue to attack us.

> Then Jesus was led up by the Spirit into the wilderness to be tempted by the devil. And when He had fasted forty days and forty nights, afterward He was hungry. Now when the tempter came to Him, he said, "If You are the son of God, command that these stones become bread." But He answered and said, "It is written, 'Man shall not live by bread alone, but by every word that proceeds from the mouth of God.'
>
> —Matthew 4:1-4 (NKJ)

There are three points that are important to note in this passage of scripture. The first thing to take note of in this scripture is that the Spirit led Jesus into the wilderness to be tempted by the devil. Jesus came to earth to be our "sacrificial lamb" and overcome the world, reconciling us back to the Father. This meant facing the temptations that came His way. "For we do not have a High Priest who cannot sympathize with our weaknesses, but was in all points tempted as we are, yet without sin" (Hebrews 4:15, NKJ). This was an important test for Jesus. Jesus needed to live a perfect life without sin. Only then could He take on the sins of the world and make atonement for us. Through the ages of time all of mankind have been and will continue to be tempted by the devil and his army. The devil is not omnipresent and cannot be everywhere at once. For most of us, we are dealing with demons or evil angels. However, the temptation will come. The bottom line is that it is the same bunch of losers that we are dealing with. Jesus has beaten them all by living a perfect life without sin and going to the cross to seal our redemption. Jesus has won the war, but we still have to fight the battles.

The second thing to notice in our reading of Matthew 4:1-4 is that the devil is referred to as the "tempter." The enemy comes to you to try to persuade you to do wrong or to provoke you into making the wrong choices that will lead you away from God. Temptation can find an open door when our mind is focused on our own desires, needs, wants, or lusts. At times, in our own unbelief, we can't imagine that God could fulfill our deepest needs or desires. The temptation, in whatever form, will offer an alternative to God's direction. This is what happened in the Garden of Eden.

> Now the serpent was more cunning than any beast of the field which the Lord God had made. And he said to the woman, "Has God indeed said, 'You shall not eat of every tree of the garden'?" And the woman said to the serpent, "We may eat the fruit of the trees of the garden; but of the fruit of the tree which is in the midst of the garden, God has said, 'You shall not eat it, nor shall you touch it, lest you die.'" Then the serpent said to the woman. "You will not surely die. For God knows that in the day you eat of it your eyes will be opened, and you will be like God, knowing good and evil." So when the woman saw that the tree was good for food, that it was pleasant to the eyes, and a tree desirable to make one wise, she took of its fruit and ate. She also gave to her husband with her, and he ate.
>
> —Genesis 3:1-6 (NKJ)

The devil suggested to Eve that the warning that God gave about eating of the fruit couldn't possibly be the absolute word on the subject. If they ate the fruit they would not die as God said they would but would be like God. This is the alternative that the devil offered Eve, and she took it and then gave

Adam the fruit to eat, as well. Notice that in the last part of the scripture it says that Eve saw that the tree was good for food, it was pleasant to the eyes, and it was desirable to make one wise; therein lies the temptation. Her senses were enticed, and she gave in to what her mind thought was the logical conclusion. After all, why would God deprive her of a good thing? The devil can tempt us in many ways. He appeals to our five senses that are within our fleshly nature, and he can appeal to the logic of our mind. The devil knows every weakness and strength that we have. He wants to gain access into our thoughts in order to plant lies against God's Word and weaken our relationship with God. If he can get us to question or doubt any part of the Word of God, he has gained a foothold in our minds.

One of the biggest lies that the devil has planted in the minds of God's children is that God doesn't love them. If you are one of the devil's victims who has believed that God doesn't love you, let me tell you plainly that God does and always will love you. His love for you will not change. Remember what we have discussed previously in this book about what the meaning of love is as described in 1 Corinthians 13? The following depicts the true love that God has for you.

> Love suffers long and is kind; love does not envy; love does not parade itself, is not puffed up; does not behave rudely, does not seek its own, is not provoked, thinks no

evil; does not rejoice in iniquity, but rejoices in the truth; bears all things, believes all things, hopes all things, endures all things. Love never fails. But whether there are prophecies, they will fail; whether there are tongues, they will cease; whether there is knowledge, it will vanish away.

—1 Corinthians 13:4-8 (NKJ)

God sent His own Son to be sacrificed so that we could have eternal life and live with Him in heaven. We have the name of Jesus, which represents the authority that has totally stripped the devil of his power by the work on the cross. We have the blood of Jesus that was shed on the cross as a sacrifice for our sins that saves us from eternal, spiritual death. If that isn't love, please tell me what is! God isn't just sitting up there in heaven, watching the enemy of our soul beat us to a pulp. Jesus has done all of the work necessary for us to resist the temptations of the devil was completed. It is so important for us to have the mind of Christ in our daily walk. God's thoughts are higher than our thoughts. Our heavenly Father sees the whole eternal picture and surely knows how to help us escape temptation or any trap of the enemy.

The third thing of significance in the scripture of Matthew 4:1-4 is that Jesus answered the devil's temptation by quoting the last part of the following scripture. In this scripture the Lord is speaking to the children of Israel and reminding them of what He has done in their lives. "So He humbled you, allowed you to hunger, and fed you with manna which you did not know nor did your fathers know, that He might make you know that man shall not live by bread alone; but by every word that proceeds from the mouth of the Lord" (Deuteronomy 8:3, NKJ).

As Jesus is our example, and since He used the Word of God to resist temptation, I would suggest that we might do the same. The words that come out of our mouths are powerful and can bless or curse mankind. Our words can even affect the spirit realm. Of course this involves more than just speaking words at random or finding a scripture and quoting it just to see if it is effective. When we speak the Word of God, for it to be effective we must speak from out of a believing heart. The Word of God is not a magical potion of any kind that can be uttered at random to achieve the desired results. Jesus believed the words that He was speaking to the devil, and so must we. This comes from having a relationship with the Lord. The devil already knows if we are carnal or spiritual, but do we know if we are carnal or spiritual? The relationship that we have with God will tell us, and the Holy Spirit will bear witness of that relationship. Luke wrote the following account in regarding to how the spirits can distinguish the difference between believers and nonbelievers.

Now God worked unusual miracles by the hands of Paul, so that even handkerchiefs or aprons were brought from his body to the sick, and the diseases left them and the evil spirits went out of them. Then some of the itinerant Jewish exorcists took it upon themselves to call the name of the Lord Jesus over those who had evil spirits, saying "We exorcise you by the Jesus whom Paul preaches." Also there were seven sons of Sceva, a Jewish chief priest, who did so. And the evil spirit answered and said, "Jesus I know, and Paul I know; but who are you?" Then the man in whom the evil spirit was leaped on them, overpowered them, and prevailed against them, so that they fled out of that house naked and wounded.

—Acts 19:11-16 (NKJ)

I suggest that when the evil spirits told the exorcists that they did not know who they were, they were not speaking literally. They were acknowledging the fact that they knew these men did not have the spiritual understanding or authority that Paul and Jesus had; therefore, the evil spirits did not have to adhere to their spoken words. In saying that, they were allowed to overcome the exorcists. Sometimes we try to use the Bible like a book of tricks. The Bible is a spiritual book. It is a book about relationships and the Love that the heavenly Father has given to us. One of the names of Jesus is "the Word." The following scripture is referring to Jesus. "And the Word became flesh and dwelt among us, and we beheld His glory, the glory as of the only begotten of the Father, full of grace and truth" (John 1:14, NKJ).

In order to confront temptation that comes our way, we need to understand that Jesus has destroyed the works of the devil and broken his power over us. "Inasmuch then as the children have partaken of flesh and blood, He Himself likewise shared in the same, that through death He might destroy him who had the power of death, that is, the devil" Hebrews 2:14, NKJ). Jesus did this work by living a perfect life without sin, becoming our sacrifice and enduring the torture of the cross and even death, resulting in His resurrection. He spilt His own blood for our sin and paid the price for all of our indiscretions and bad decisions. God is holy and holiness demands justice. Remember when we talked about God being holy and also merciful? These two attributes flow from a God who is the very meaning and essence of love. So if Jesus has already done all the work, what is left for us to do? Jesus is speaking in the following scripture. "Behold, I give you the authority to trample on serpents and scorpions, and over all the power of the enemy, and nothing shall by any means hurt you" (Luke 10:19, NKJ).

Jesus, having won the war for us, has given us the authority to overcome the power of the devil. We are left to carry on with the battles of everyday life. We are back to making the right choices on a daily basis and aligning those choices with the will and Word of God in our lives. "Therefore submit to God. Resist the devil and he will flee from you" (James 4:7, NKJ). Let's take this scripture to a personal level. We need to make the choice to resist temptation and put down our flesh, not regarding the situation as it looks in the natural. Speak to that situation (or spirit) just like Jesus did when he confronted the devil. Having the mind of Christ, let the Spirit of God arise within you and help you rebuke (resist) any demonic or evil attack. You have the Holy Spirit within you, the name of Jesus, and the blood of Jesus. Have faith in God and believe that your heavenly Father will do what He says He will do. What more do you need? Evil powers know when you are filled with faith and with the Word of God. See beyond the natural situation and see what God is doing on a much higher level and purpose. Life passes so quickly on this earth—here today and gone tomorrow. God sees you on an eternal level. As an eternal being, you need to see more than just a short-term vision of what your life consists of.

Temptation started in the Garden of Eden. The "tempter," known as the devil, came to Eve and told her that even though God had told them not to eat the fruit of the tree of the knowledge of good and evil, if she ate the fruit she would be like God, knowing good and evil. Eve ate of the fruit of the tree, and so did Adam, bringing the curse upon the earth. Spiritual and physical death then came upon the earth and every living creature, as well. God wants us to serve him out of love and of our own free will. The devil wants to make slaves of us.

Satan once was a cherub, an anointed angel of God who ministered upon the holy mountain of God, where the very throne of God exists. Pride was found in him, and he wanted to be like God. He was kicked out of heaven along with the angels who followed him. Since then in his rebellion, he has tried to destroy and lead mankind away from God. The devil comes to kill, steal, and destroy. He and his army of demons and evil angels will distort the Word of God and use any weakness that he sees in us for his advantage. He will use any weakness in our flesh, any pain we may be carrying, or any anger that we may be harboring. He will use our friends, enemies, or any circumstance to take advantage. He wants a foothold into our thought life to start planting doubt and lies about our God and our relationship with Him. The devil is the enemy of our soul.

The good news is that Jesus has stripped the devil of his power over us. Jesus has overcome the world by overcoming evil with good. We fight our battles daily, but Jesus has won the war. It is up to us to resist the devil, and he will flee from us. It all comes to the choices that we make just as Adam and Eve had choices to make. Jesus has given us the authority to overcome the enemy of our soul. We have the mind of Christ, and just like Jesus we can use the Word of God to resist and make the devil flee from us. We have the name of Jesus (that represents the authority that was given to us) to overcome the enemy. We have the blood of Jesus (that was sacrificed for our sins) that puts us in right standing with God. The devil would like to get our focus off of God, keeping us focused on our immediate needs and situations in our lives. If he can get us into the fear and panic mode, by separating us from God and His Word, then we are bound to make the wrong decisions that leave us open for an attack from the enemy of our soul. God is working in our lives for eternal purposes. God has promised us that he will make a way of escape from our temptation and that we will not be tempted beyond what we can bear. One of the biggest lies that the devil has is that God doesn't love you. God will always love you, and He will never stop loving you because God *is* love.

THE LOVE OF
THE FATHER

*W*e were all created for a definite purpose, which is of our own free will, to love and serve our Creator and lover of our soul. "Jesus said to him, 'You shall love the Lord your God with all your heart, with all your soul, and with all your mind. This is the first and great commandment. And the second is like it: 'You shall love your neighbor as yourself'" (Matthew 22:37-39, NKJ). Remember, God *is* love. If you have ever wondered why you were created, I suggest that it is for this purpose. The Father God wants to have a relationship of love with each of His children, including you. God's plans for you are bigger than you could have ever imagined. "But as it is written: Eye has not seen, nor ear heard, nor have entered into the heart of man the things

which God has prepared for those who love Him"
(1 Corinthians 2:9, NKJ).

In order to understand the love of the Father
toward us, we need a revelation in our hearts
of what really took place in Genesis with Adam
and Eve in the Garden of Eden. In the following
scripture God is speaking to Adam and Eve.

> Then God blessed them, and God said to
> them, "Be fruitful and multiply; fill the
> earth and subdue it; have dominion over
> the fish of the sea, over the birds of the air,
> and over every living thing that moves on
> the earth." And God said, "See I have given
> you every herb that yields seed which is
> on the face of all the earth, and every tree
> whose fruit yields seed; to you it shall be
> for food. Also, to every beast of the earth, to
> every bird of the air, and to everything that
> creeps on the earth, in which there is life, I
> have given every green herb for food"; and
> it was so."
>
> —Genesis 1:28-30 (NKJ)

Everything that God had created and made was
perfect. God then gave this gift of the earth and
all that was created and made in it to Adam and
Eve and their descendents (that means you). He
also gave them (and us) dominion over the earth.
They were appointed to be the caretakers over

the earth. This perfect creation was what God wanted mankind to have and enjoy. God intended for mankind to take care of the earth and have supreme authority and dominion over every living thing that moves on the earth, including the birds in the air. Mankind was also given every herb and seed, as well as every tree with its fruit and seed. Does this not demonstrate the love of the Father for mankind? Everything that man could possibly need, God had provided. Death and decay were not on God's agenda for mankind. He only desired, and still does desire, good things for His children.

> Then the Lord God took the man and put him in the garden of Eden to tend and keep it. And the Lord God commanded the man, saying, "Of every tree of the garden you may freely eat; but of the tree of the knowledge of good and evil you shall not eat, for in the day that you eat of it you shall surely die.
>
> —Genesis 2:15-17

In this statement God gave man a choice. God gave man everything he could possibly need and did not withhold anything except eating from the tree of the knowledge of good and evil. Why would God do that? God did not want a group of robots serving him, but he wanted man to serve him of his own choice, his own free will. This is what true love and relationships are about. God wanted children, not slaves. Therefore, choices had to be a part of the equation.

True love does not seek its own will. The serpent now enters our scene in the Garden of Eden. He tempts Eve into eating of the fruit of the tree of the knowledge of good and evil by telling her that she would be like God, knowing good and evil. She eats the fruit of the tree and gives Adam the fruit to eat, as well, thus sealing the fate of mankind. In the following scripture God speaks to the snake (the reptile) because this was the form that Satan used to deceive Eve. God then speaks to Satan and foretells his end and the coming of Jesus who will defeat him. Eve is addressed next and then Adam. God lets them know that there will be consequences of having eaten the forbidden fruit.

> So the Lord God said to the serpent: "Because you have done this, you are cursed more than all cattle, and more than every beast of the field; on your belly you shall go, and you shall eat dust all the days of your life. And I will put enmity between you and the woman, and between your seed and her Seed; He shall bruise your head, and you shall bruise His heel." To the woman He said: "I will greatly multiply your sorrow and your conception; in pain you shall bring forth children; your desire shall be for your husband, and he shall rule

over you." Then to Adam He said, "Because you have heeded the voice of your wife, and have eaten from the tree of which I commanded you, saying, 'You shall not eat of it': Cursed is the ground for your sake; in toil you shall eat of it all the days of your life. Both thorns and thistles it shall bring forth for you, and you shall eat the herb of the field. In the sweat of your face you shall eat bread till you return to the ground, for out of it you were taken; for dust you are, and to dust you shall return.

—Genesis 3:14-19 (NKJ)

This is how the curse came upon the earth and physical death, as well as spiritual death, began to work in the world that God had created. It was not what God wanted, but it was what man had chosen. God honored Adam's choice just as He honors the choices each of us make in our lives even when they are the wrong choices. In the previous scripture, God laid out the consequences of the choice that Adam, who represented the human race, had made. God was not the one who corrupted the earth. However, God did make a way of escape for mankind from spiritual death.

When God is speaking to the Serpent, He mentions that there is enmity between the Serpent and the woman, her Seed and his seed. Notice that the word "Seed" pertaining to the woman is capitalized. This "Seed of the woman" is in reference to Jesus Christ. This is marking a definite difference between the two. The scripture goes on to say that the Seed of the woman shall bruise the Serpent's (Satan), head and the Serpent shall bruise His heel. This is in reference to the cross, death, burial, and resurrection of the Lord Jesus Christ. This is our hope for the ages. The promise of the Messiah had been given. "For God so love the world that He gave His only begotten Son, that whoever believes in Him should not perish but have everlasting life" (John 3:16, NKJ). This is the action of a loving God who cares for His children. God had created a perfect world for man to live in and did not deny him anything only to ask him to not eat of the forbidden fruit in the Garden of Eden. Eve was tempted, and Adam chose to eat of the fruit. Even when the wrong choice was made by Adam and Eve, God made a way of escape for mankind by promising us that the Messiah would come to break the power of the curse and save mankind "For as in Adam all die, even so in Christ all shall be made alive" (1 Corinthians 15:22, NKJ). Even though "the curse" is still at work in the earth, the power of Satan has been broken. If we believe in God's Son, Jesus Christ, we will have eternal life with the heavenly Father, which He has desired throughout the ages of time. The love of the Father has not waivered for His children in all of this.

How are you feeling right now about how the Father loves you? Some of us blame God for so many things going wrong in the earth, and we want Him to intervene and make it all the way it should be. One day in the near future that will indeed be the case. Jesus is going to come back and make right all of the wrongs that have happened from the beginning of time. God has His own time frame of when all of these things will come to pass. In the meantime, we must fight the battle and run our race of life on a daily basis. The curse is still at work in the earth. Satan is still coming around to tempt us (just as he did with Adam and Eve) and trying to trap and draw us away from the heavenly Father who loves us. The war of good and evil continues. The battles we fight in our daily lives make us stronger and reinforce our love and faith in our God. It is critical for us to understand what happened in the Garden of Eden and the resulting consequences of the choices that Adam and Eve made, which still affects our lives. God's plan for man has not changed. His love for us has not changed. He still wants a family that wants to love Him and to be with Him. Heaven is eternal and we have a spirit in us that is eternal, making us eternal beings. Where we spend eternity is based on the decisions that we make down here. The life that we live down here is fleeting compared to eternity, so make your choices in life with eternity in mind.

God did not abandon us after the Garden of Eden. He chose a people from the seed of Abraham, who would be known later as "Jews," to represent Him in the earth. If they would follow

His commandments and worship Him, they would be blessed. This race would bring forth the Messiah who would save all of mankind and reconcile them, and all the generations that would follow, back to the Father. This would enable the Father to go on with His original plan of having a people to love and worship Him and who would live with Him in heaven. The Jewish people would be a nation in which God could demonstrate His love and power in the earth. God instituted the blood sacrifice as a way to make atonement for the sins of the people. God is holy, and sin must be atoned by blood because the life force is in the blood. The blood sacrifice was temporal because the blood was only animal blood and not pure enough to abolish sin. Therefore, sacrifices were made often as man was continually sinning. God also instituted a temple for the people to come to worship Him.

There were several laws and rites that had to be kept in order to keep the presence of God among the people. These laws and commandments of God separated the Jews from the rest of mankind. They were known as the "people of the living God" and were feared among their enemies. God was giving a demonstration in the earth of what He would do if people would worship and love Him. Even with all of the miracles that were performed in the Old Testament, people still did not want to serve God. God's love was still with man, but mankind did not want Him. Mankind wanted to choose their own way and not do as God would have them do. As a result, the world was in a terrible state and still is to this day. We squander the world's resources, and our corruption spreads from generation to generation. Our heavenly Father's love was, and still is, reaching down to make a way for man, but like Adam, man keeps disobeying God and choosing to do things his own way, which always leads to death and destruction in one form or another.

Finally, the time came for the Messiah, Jesus Christ, to come to earth. Jesus came to earth at the request of the heavenly Father. Jesus said that He came to do the will of the Father, not His own will. Jesus is speaking in the following scripture.

> For I have come down from heaven, not to do My own will, but the will of Him who sent Me. This is the will of the Father who sent Me, that of all He has given Me I should lose nothing, but should raise it up at the last day. And this is the will of Him who sent Me, that everyone who sees the Son and believes in Him may have everlasting life; and I will raise him up at the last day.
>
> —John 6:38-40 (NKJ)

The words and the works that Jesus did on this earth were done by the heavenly Father who dwelt in Jesus. Jesus was obedient and submitted to His

Father. How much more should we submit to the heavenly Father? Jesus was the perfect sacrifice that was made for mankind. Jesus lived a perfect life and the blood that flowed through His veins was perfect and could atone once and for all for the sins of mankind, not only for then, but for now and forever. This was and is the ultimate love sacrifice that the Father made for His creation. Can we even begin to imagine or comprehend the kind of great love that it took for God and Jesus to make this sacrifice? Jesus was God's own Son. He was an eternal Spirit who has always been in existence with the Father. He took the form of man with all of the pain, struggles, and poverty that life brings. Jesus successfully faced not only the temptations of Satan but also the trials of everyday life.

In the lifetime of Jesus the Jews were slaves of the Roman Empire. Life could be unbearable, and death was always close at hand. Even the religious people hated Jesus. They were jealous of the miracles He did and saw Him as a threat to their way of existence. They taunted and came at Him on a daily basis to try to trip Him up in His teachings. Can you imagine how this could wear a normal person down? Jesus was a perfect man, and yet imperfection was all around Him. This is why Jesus is our High Priest. He understands what we are going through and is able to intercede for us to the Father. Can you see that God is still reaching down to us with that same perfect love and intent that He had for Adam? God is not our enemy. Jesus had to face life's trials, and so will we. The love of the Father reached down to us through Jesus, and when Jesus went back to heaven, the Holy Spirit came to dwell within man. God did not at any time abandon mankind. Jesus is speaking of the Holy Spirit in the following scripture.

> Nevertheless I tell you the truth. It is to your advantage that I go away; for if I do not go away, the Helper will not come to you; but if I depart, I will send Him to you. And when He has come, He will convict the world of sin, and of righteousness, and of judgment: of sin, because they do not believe in Me; of righteousness, because I go to My Father and you see me no more; of judgment, because the ruler of this world is judged. I still have many things to say to you, but you cannot bear them now. However, when He, the Spirit of truth, has come, He will guide you into all truth; for He will not speak on His own authority, but whatever He hears He will speak; and He will tell you things to come. He will glorify Me, for He will take of what is Mine and declare it to you. All things that the Father has are Mine. Therefore I said that He will take of Mine and declare it to you.

> —John 16:7-15 (NKJ)

Jesus was one man and could only minister to a few people at a time. The Holy Spirit came to dwell within each of us. God has manifested His love for and to us by giving us the Helper to guide us and teach us about the kingdom of God. Jesus is speaking in the following scripture.

> But the Comforter (Counselor, Helper, Intercessor, Advocate, Strengthener, Standby), the Holy Spirit, Whom the father will send in My name [in My place, to represent Me and act on My behalf], He will teach you all things. And He will cause you to recall—will remind you of, bring to your remembrance—everything I have told you.
>
> —John 14:26 (Amplified)

As we yield ourselves to the Spirit of God within us, we become one with the Father, fulfilling His desire to have a family that willingly loves and serves Him. The Holy Spirit will lead, guide, and direct us in our daily lives, showing us the will of the Father. As we yield ourselves to God, our lives become as a beacon of light in a dark world for all to see and glorify God. The Holy Spirit is here to help us in times of suffering and fear. By the Spirit of God we can overcome all the works of the flesh and face any temptation that the devil can throw at us in victory. By the Spirit of

God, we can forgive those people who have hurt us. The love of the Father has remained and will remain a constant from the beginning of time and throughout eternity.

How about you? If you have accepted Jesus as Lord and Savior you are a part of the family of God and His kingdom. How are you feeling about the love that the Father has for you? God loves you. He cannot and will not ever stop loving you. There is nothing that you have done or ever will do that will make Him stop loving you.

If you have lived a life of fear, abuse, or failure, God is still with you. He never has left you. It breaks His heart to see the pain and suffering that you have been through. It was not His will that you had to cry so many tears or go through the suffering and humiliation that life has offered up to you. Life isn't fair, but you can rest assured that one day God will balance the books on injustice. Jesus is speaking in the following scripture. "These things I have spoken to you, that in Me you may have peace. In the world you will have tribulation; but be of good cheer, I have overcome the world" (John 16:33, NKJ).

Jesus had tribulation in this world, and so will you. Jesus didn't come and overthrow the Roman government even though the Jews, during the life of Jesus, were slaves to the Romans. Life was hard and persecution was a daily event for many of the people. Jesus dealt with the hearts of men. He is dealing with your heart right now. What is

He saying to you? God wants to heal your broken heart. Call out to Him, and He will answer you. He wants to reveal the principles of His kingdom to you. Let God by His Holy Spirit walk with you as you continue your life's journey. You will not be disappointed.

What if you haven't accepted Jesus as Lord and Savior? I have some good news for you. The apostle Paul is speaking in the following scripture.

> Because if you acknowledge and confess with your lips that Jesus is Lord and in your heart believe (adhere to, trust in and rely on the truth) that God raised Him from the dead, you will be saved. For with the heart a person believes (adheres to, trusts in and relies on Christ) and so is justified (declared righteous, acceptable to God), and with the mouth he confesses—declares openly and speaks out freely his faith—and confirms [his] salvation.
>
> —Romans 10:9-10 (Amplified)

It is important to God that mankind chooses to serve and love Him of his own free will. It is a choice that every individual has to make and the outcome of that decision will have eternal ramifications. God does not force you into heaven, nor will He force you into hell. Your eternal destination is a result of your own choice.

Mankind was constantly making the wrong choices and sinning against God, who is holy. The penalty for sin is eternal death. Jesus came to pay that price. Jesus is the only one that could fulfill such a sacrifice. The prophet Isaiah wrote a prophecy about Jesus coming here to earth and of His mission.

> He is despised and rejected by men, a Man of sorrows and acquainted with grief. And we hid, as it were, our faces from Him; He was despised, and we did not esteem Him. Surely He has borne our griefs and carried our sorrows; yet we esteemed Him stricken, smitten by God, and afflicted. But He was wounded for our transgressions, He was bruised for our iniquities; the chastisement for our peace was upon Him, and by His stripes we are healed. All we like sheep have gone astray; we have turned, everyone, to his own way; and the Lord has laid on Him the iniquity of us all. He was oppressed and He was afflicted, yet He opened not His mouth; He was led as a lamb to the slaughter, and as a sheep before its shearers is silent, so He opened not His mouth. He was taken from prison and from judgment, and who will declare His generation? For He was cut off from the land of the living; for the transgressions of My people He was stricken. And they made His grave

with the wicked—but with the rich at His death, because He had done no violence, nor was any deceit in His mouth. Yet it pleased the Lord to bruise Him; He has put Him to grief. When You make His soul an offering for sin, He shall see His seed, He shall prolong His days, and the pleasure of the Lord shall prosper in His hand. He shall see the labor of His soul, and be satisfied. By His knowledge My righteous Servant shall justify many, for He shall bear their iniquities. Therefore I will divide Him a portion with the great, and He shall divide the spoil with the strong, because He poured out His soul unto death, and He was numbered with the transgressors, and He bore the sin of many, and made intercession for the transgressors.

—Isaiah 53:3-12 (NKJ)

The Lord is not the cause of all your problems. God has not abandoned you. He has never left you. God has always, since the beginning of time, found a way to send His love to you and find a way of escape from eternal death and separation from Him. God is not indifferent to what you are going through in your life. He is not sitting in heaven, waiting for a chance to punish you or finding a way to make life more difficult for you. The opposite is true. God and Jesus want you to be blessed and have joy. Please, do not blame God for the sorrow and hurt that has happened in your life. Accept the love of the Father in the gift of Jesus the Christ and let Him heal your brokenness and restore you to all of the potential He has created in you. After all, life is eternal.

If you haven't received Jesus as Lord and Savior and are ready now, please pray the following prayer.

> Dear heavenly Father, I believe that Jesus is the Son of God and that He came to earth to take away the sins of the world, and that also includes my sins. I confess and renounce my sins and I accept Jesus as my Savior and Lord. Jesus, I ask you to come into my heart and become Lord over my life. Empower me by the Holy Spirit that dwells in me to live for you and testify of your love to others. In Jesus's name I pray. Amen.

You are a part of the family of God, the body of Christ. If you currently do not belong to a church, I encourage you to pray and ask the Holy Spirit to show you where to find a home church. In a home church, you can grow in the love and the fellowship of other people who can share your faith. Attend church regularly so that you may grow in the Word of God.

As a final note to all of you, God loves you so much! He will never stop loving you. He will never leave you or forsake you. Do not be afraid. You are not alone. You never were, and you never will be. I am so glad that you took time to read this book. I hope it has encouraged and helped you in your relationship with your heavenly Father. Now I would like to leave you with a blessing. "The Lord bless you and keep you; the Lord make His face to shine upon you, and be gracious to you; the Lord lift up His countenance upon you, and give you peace" (Numbers 6:24-26, NKJ).

Remember, nothing is or can be as great to you as the perfect love of the Father.